BRITANNICA'S PRACTICAL GUIDE TO THE ARTS

PAINTING

MATERIALS, TECHNIQUES, STYLES, AND PRACTICE

EDITED BY
DENIS E. McGUINNESS

Britannica
Educational Publishing

IN ASSOCIATION WITH

ROSEN
EDUCATIONAL SERVICES

Published in 2017 by Britannica Educational Publishing (a trademark of Encyclopædia Britannica, Inc.) in association with The Rosen Publishing Group, Inc.
29 East 21st Street, New York, NY 10010

Distributed exclusively by Rosen Publishing.
To see additional Britannica Educational Publishing titles, go to rosenpublishing.com.

First Edition

Britannica Educational Publishing
J.E. Luebering: Executive Director, Core Editorial
Anthony L. Green: Editor, Compton's by Britannica

Rosen Publishing
Kathy Kuhtz Campbell: Senior Editor
Nelson Sá: Art Director
Michael Moy: Designer
Cindy Reiman: Photography Manager
Nicole Baker: Photo Researcher
Supplementary material by Denis E. McGuinness

Library of Congress Cataloging-in-Publication Data

Names: McGuinness, Denis E. editor.
Title: Painting : materials, techniques, styles, and practice / Edited by Denis E. McGuinness.
Description: New York : Britannica Educational Pub. in Association with Rosen Educational Services, 2017. | Series: Britannica's Practical Guide to the Arts | Includes bibliographical references and index.
Identifiers: LCCN 2015046452 | ISBN 9781680483734 (library bound : alk. paper)
Subjects: LCSH: Painting--Technique--Juvenile literature. | Artists' materials--Juvenile literature.
Classification: LCC ND1471 .P355 2016 | DDC 751.4--dc23
LC record available at http://lccn.loc.gov/2015046452

Manufactured in China

Photo credits: Cover (inset images, from left) George Dolgikh/Shutterstock.com, avs/Shutterstock.com, bikeriderlondon/Shutterstock.com; cover (background), p. i lady.diana/Shutterstock.com; pp. iii, viii-ix (background) maxim ibragimov/Shutterstock.com; p. ix (inset) Munson-Williams-Proctor Arts Institute/Art Resource, NY; pp. 1, 67 Getty Images; p. 3 Photograph, courtesy of Giraudon—Art Resource, New York; pp. 9. 11,15, Encyclopædia Britannica, Inc.; p. 17 DEA Picture Library/Getty Images; 35 Foto Marburg/Art Resource, New York; p. 41 Apic/Hulton Fine Art Collection/Getty Images; p. 43 ullstein bild/Getty Images; p. 44 Courtesy of the Victoria and Albert Museum, London. Photograph, John Webb; p. 47 Sean Gallup/Getty Images; p. 52 Board of Trustees of the National Museums and Galleries in Merseyside (Walker Art Gallery Liverpool); pp. 54, 57 Mondadori Portfolio/Getty Images; p. 59 Javier Sánchez/Moment/Getty Images; p. 62 Library of Congress, Washington, D.C. (neg. no. LC-USZ62-117437); p. 72 Museo Thyssen-Bornemisza/Scala/Art Resource, NY; p. 83 SuperStock/Getty Images; p. 90 Jason Kempin/Getty Images; p. 95 SCALA/Art Resource, New York; p. 97 Mario Tama/Getty Images; p. 103 Courtesy of the Victoria and Albert Museum, London; p. 107 Photos.com/Thinkstock; p. 109 National Palace Museum, Taipei, Taiwan; pp. 140, 164 Universal History Archive/Universal Images Group/Getty Images; p. 145 Courtesy of the Rijksmuseum, Amsterdam; on loan from the City of Amsterdam; p. 151 Image © 2004 Board of Trustees, National Gallery of Art, Washington, D.C., Widener Collection, photograph, Richard Carafelli; p. 159 Courtesy of the Albertina, Vienna; p. 174 Galleria Sabauda, Turin, Italy/Bridgeman Images; p. 178 P. Chandra; p. 182 small_frog/E+/Getty Images; back cover and interior pages stripe pattern Eky Studio/Shutterstock.com; additional cover and interior page border patterns and textures Dragana Jokmanovic//Shutterstock.com, somchaiP//Shutterstock.com, Alina G//Shutterstock.com, Pattanawit Chan//Shutterstock.com

CHAPTER SEVEN

INTRODUCTION

The fine arts are modes of expression that use skill or imagination in the creation of aesthetic objects, environments, or experiences that can be shared with others. Traditional categories within the arts include literature, visual arts (painting, drawing, sculpture, etc.), graphic arts (painting, drawing, design, and other forms expressed on flat surfaces), plastic arts (sculpture, modeling), decorative arts (enamel work, furniture design, mosaic, etc.), performing arts, music, and architecture. The fine art of painting is as varied as the life from which it springs. Each artist portrays different aspects of the world. A great artist is able to take some aspect of life and give it depth and meaning. To do this he or she will make use of the many devices common to painting. These devices include composition (the arrangement of the objects within a picture), colour, form, and texture.

A painter does not always need handsome and attractive subjects. Often an ordinary subject is transformed through artistry. The painting *November Evening* by American artist Charles Burchfield depicts simple homes and stores typical of many crossroads towns in the Midwest in the 1930s. Beyond the buildings stretches the vast prairie set against a single human figure. A dark autumn sky covers the landscape.

Burchfield has given the scene dignity through his honest and open treatment. He has not tried to make the picture pretty by hiding the poor proportions of the buildings or their ungainly grouping. By stressing the contrast

I. Rice Pereira's *Vacillating Progression* (1949) is an abstract work in which the artist applied oil and plastic paints on glass.

between the huddled buildings and the great open spaces surrounding them, he gives a feeling of warm human companionship. Land and sky rule the lives of the people in this little community. The buildings reflect the curve of the swell of land on which they rest, as the windows reflect the light of the evening sky. Yet, for all its awkwardness and clumsiness, the town still maintains a simple dignity.

Hopscotch (1940) is another painting of an unexpected subject. American painter Loren MacIver has set down on canvas a small fragment of the world—a patch of asphalt on which some children have been playing. From this simple source, she has discovered a world of wonder. The asphalt is no longer just a common material with which streets are paved but a substance of fascinating and varied shapes and rich textures. It is a playground for children. The regular chalked lines of the hopscotch are an interesting contrast to the free, irregular shapes of the pavement. In this small scene the observer also gets some hint of the forces of the world, especially of nature. The paving material has bubbled and eroded because of the action of sun, rain, and frost. MacIver has shown that even a commonplace subject has beauty.

Some artists use geometric or abstract forms, colours, and textures to create interest and meaning. Most music does not attempt to imitate natural sounds, and there is no reason why painting should always make use of nature. *White Lines* (1942), by American artist I. Rice Pereira, is an example of such nonobjective painting. Pereira has constructed her picture entirely with lines and rectangles of different shapes, sizes, colours, and textures. The rectangles appear on top of and next to each other. This is a study in patterns. Like music, it creates beauty from rhythm and harmony.

Briefly it may be said that artists paint to discover truth and to create order. They put into their pictures people's common hopes, ideals, and passions, and show them their meaning and their value. Creators in all the arts make discoveries about the wonders and beauties of nature and the dignity and nobility of humankind. They give these an order that enables people to see and understand life with greater depth. Beauty generally results from order but as a by-product, not a primary aim. Not all works of art are beautiful.

In the early part of the 20th century, a group of American artists called the Ashcan School began painting unglamorous scenes of industrial subjects such as railroad tracks and factories. John Sloan, Robert Henri, George Bellows, and George Luks were prominent members of this group. At the time, these pictures of city life were considered ugly and offensive. Yet these pioneers discovered in such subjects much that was beautiful. Today it is commonly accepted that industrial scenes are rich sources of pleasure in art. It was the artist, perceptive and sensitive, who discovered new areas of enjoyment.

The painter is able to intensify individuals' experiences. By finding new relationships among objects, new forms, and new colours, painters show people things in their environment that they have overlooked or ignored. Painters make the encompassing world become alive, rich, beautiful, and exciting.

The subject that an artist selects for a painting depends largely upon the time in which that person lives. A painter living in the Middle Ages would probably have picked a religious subject, because that was almost the only topic portrayed at the time. Had he lived in Holland during the 17th century he might have painted portraits, family scenes, or arrangements of dishes, fruits, and flowers, called still lifes.

At the present time few artists are painting religious pictures, and portraiture is less prevalent than it was once. Many new subjects have become available. The airplane has inspired artists to work on problems of space. The increasing use of machines has led painters to study mechanical forms. Abstract and nonobjective subjects seek to find some basis of order in a rapidly changing world.

In particular, modern painters were concerned with painting the inner world of thoughts, feelings, and dreams. This inner world draws upon very different forms and relationships from the outer world of reality. Such pictures can sometimes appear strange and difficult to understand. Paul Klee's *Intention* (1938) and Salvador Dalí's *The Persistence of Memory* (1931) are examples.

Having selected a subject, the painter is faced with the problem of giving it form. Will the idea be communicated best by the use of realistic or abstract forms? Should it be done in bright or in dull colours? Should the effect be exciting or restful? The answer depends upon what the painter is trying to do. In a good painting everything in it grows out of and develops from the intent of the artist.

Shapes, lines, colours, tones, and textures—the elements that make up a two-dimensional visual language—are used in various ways to produce sensations of volume, space, movement, and light on a flat surface. These elements are combined into expressive patterns to represent real or supernatural phenomena, to interpret a narrative theme, or to create wholly abstract visual relationships. An artist's decision to use a particular medium, such as tempera, fresco, oil, acrylic, watercolour or other water-based paints, ink, gouache, encaustic, or casein, as well as the choice of a particular form, such as mural, easel, panel, miniature, manuscript illumination, scroll, screen or fan, panorama, or any of a variety of modern forms, is based on the sensuous qualities and the expressive possibilities and limitations of those options. The choices of the medium and the form, as well as the artist's own technique, combine to realize a unique visual image.

Earlier cultural traditions—of tribes, religions, guilds, royal courts, and states—largely controlled the craft, form, imagery, and subject matter of painting and determined its function, whether ritualistic, devotional, decorative, entertaining, or educational. Painters were employed more as skilled artisans than as creative artists. Later, the notion of the "fine artist" developed in Asia and Renaissance Europe. Prominent painters were afforded the social status of scholars and courtiers; they signed their work, decided its design and often its subject and imagery, and they established a more personal—if not always amicable—relationship with their patrons.

During the 19th century, painters in Western societies began to lose their social positions and secure patronages. Some artists countered the decline in patronage support by holding their own exhibitions and charging entrance fees. Others earned an income through touring exhibitions of their work. The need to appeal to a marketplace had replaced the similar (if less impersonal) demands of patronage; its effect on the art itself was probably similar as well. Generally, artists can now reach an audience through commercial galleries, public museums, art periodicals, art fairs, online sites, and social media. They may also be assisted by financial awards or commissions from industry and the state. They have, however, gained the freedom to invent their own visual language and to experiment with new forms and unconventional materials and techniques. For example, some painters have combined other media, such as sculpture, with painting to produce three-dimensional abstract designs. Other artists have attached real objects to the canvas in collage fashion or used electricity to operate coloured kinetic panels and boxes. Conceptual artists frequently express their ideas in the form of a proposal for an unrealizable project, while performance artists are an integral part of their own compositions. The restless endeavour to extend the boundaries of expression in Western art produces continuous international stylistic changes. The often bewildering succession of new movements in painting is further stimulated by the swift interchange of ideas by means of international art journals, traveling exhibitions, art centers, and social media and blogs.

Painting: Materials, Technique, Styles, and Practice is concerned with the elements and principles of design in painting and with the various mediums, forms, imagery, subject matter, and symbolism employed, adopted, or created by the painter.

THE ELEMENTS AND PRINCIPLES OF DESIGN IN PAINTING

The design of a painting is its visual format: the arrangement of its lines, shapes, colours, tones, and textures into an expressive pattern. It is the sense of inevitability in this formal organization that gives a great painting its self-sufficiency and presence.

The colours and placing of the principal images in a design may sometimes be largely decided by representational and symbolic considerations. Yet it is the formal interplay of colours and shapes that alone is capable of communicating a particular mood, producing optical sensations of space, volume, movement, and light, and creating

In *Nonchaloir (Repose)* (1911) John Singer Sargent evokes fabric textures, light reflections, and sumptuous furnishings.

forces of both harmony and tension, even when a painting's narrative symbolism is obscure.

DESIGN ELEMENTS

Each of the design elements has special expressive qualities.

LINE

Line is an intuitive, primeval convention for representing things; the simple linear imagery of young children's drawings and prehistoric rock paintings is universally understood. The formal relationships of thick with thin lines, of broken with continuous, and of sinuous with jagged are forces of contrast and repetition in the design of many paintings in all periods of history. Variations in the painted contours of images also provide a direct method of describing the volume, weight, spatial position, light, and textural characteristics of things. The finest examples of this pictorial shorthand are found in Japanese ink painting, where an expressive economy and vitality of line is closely linked to a traditional mastery of calligraphy.

In addition to painted contours, a linear design is composed of all of the edges of tone and colour masses, of the axial directions of images, and of the lines that are implied by the alignment of shapes across the picture. The manner in which these various kinds of line are echoed and repeated animates the design. The artist, whether acting consciously or intuitively, also places them in relationship to one another across the picture, so that they weave a unifying rhythmic network throughout the painting.

Apart from the obvious associations of some linear patterns with particular actions—undulating lines suggesting buoyant movement, for instance—emotive sensations are produced by certain linear relationships. Thus, lines moving upward express feelings of joy and aspiration, those directing the eye downward evoke moods of sadness or defeat, while lines at angles opening to the right are more agreeable and welcoming than those spreading outward to the left.

Leonardo's *Virgin and Child with St. Anne* (c. 1502–1516) has shapes that direct a viewer's eye in specific directions.

SHAPE AND MASS

Shape and mass, as elements of design, include all areas of different colour, tone, and texture, as well as individual and grouped images.

Children instinctively represent the things they see by geometric symbols. Not only have sophisticated modern artists, such as Paul Klee and Jean Dubuffet, borrowed this untutored imagery, but the more arresting and expressive shapes and masses in most styles of painting, and those to which most people intuitively respond, will generally be found to have been clearly based on such archetypal forms. A square or a circle will tend to dominate a design and will therefore often be found at its focal centre—the square window framing Christ in Leonardo da Vinci's *Last Supper* (1495–1498),

ADOLPH GOTTLIEB

American painter Adolph Gottlieb (1903–1974) was important as an early and outstanding member of the New York school of Abstract Expressionists.

After studying at the Art Students League of New York and in Paris, Gottlieb returned to New York in 1923 to attend Parsons School of Design, Cooper Union, and the Educational Alliance Art School.

Early in the 1940s Gottlieb developed his pictograph style, in which cryptic forms, often derived from mythology and primitive art, were used in a rectilinear, gridlike pattern. Characteristic examples are *Evil Omen* (1946) and *Romanesque Façade* (1949). During the 1950s he painted abstract landscapes, which, in turn, led to his second principal style, called "bursts," in which sunlike, static orbs float above jagged areas. The lower element was often made up of smears, blots, and other forms characteristic of action painting. The paintings became simpler and more monumental and used a limited number of colours. Examples are *Triad* (1959), *Expanding* (1962), and *Orb* (1964).

for example, the hovering sun in an Adolph Gottlieb abstract, or the halo encircling a Christian or Buddhist deity. A firmly based triangular image or shape seems reassuring, even uplifting, while the precarious balance implied by an inverted triangular shape or mass produces feelings of tension. Oval, lozenge, and rectangular forms suggest stability and protection, and they often surround vulnerable figures in narrative paintings.

There is generally a cellular unity, or family likeness, between the shapes and masses in a design similar to the visual harmony of all units to the whole observed in natural forms—the gills, fins, and scales in character with the overall shape of a fish, for example.

The negative spaces between shapes and masses are also carefully considered by the artist, since they can be adjusted to enhance the action and character of the positive images. They can be as important to the design as time intervals in music or the voids of an architectural facade.

COLOUR

In many styles and periods of painting, the functions of colour are primarily decorative and descriptive, often serving merely to reinforce the expression of an idea or subject communicated primarily through line and tone. In much of modern painting, however, the full-spectrum range of available pigments has allowed artists to use colour as the primary expressive element.

The principal dimensions of colour in painting are hue, tone, and intensity. Red, yellow, and blue are the basic hues from which all others on the chromatic scale can be made by mixtures. These three opaque hues are the subtractive pigment primaries and should not be confused with the behavior of the additive triads and mixtures of transparent, coloured light. Primary pair mixtures produce the secondary hues orange, violet, and green. By increasing the amount of one primary in each of these mixtures, the tertiary colours of yellow-orange, orange-red, red-violet, violet-blue, blue-green, and green-yellow are made. The primary colours, with their basic secondary and tertiary mixtures, can be usefully notated in 12 segments of a circle. The secondary and tertiary colour segments between a pair of primaries share a family relationship with one another—the yellow-orange, orange, and orange-red hues that lie between yellow and red, for example.

Local hues are the inherent and associative colours of things. In everyday life, familiar things are described by particular colours, and these often are identified by reference to familiar things; the green of grass and the grass green of paint, for instance. Although, as the Impressionists demonstrated, the inherent colours of forms in the real world are usually changed by effects of light and atmosphere, many of the great "primitive" and classical styles of representational painting are expressed in terms of local hues.

Tone is a colour's relative degree, or value, of lightness or darkness. The tonal pattern of a painting is shown in a monochrome reproduction. A painting dominated by dark colours, such as a Rembrandt, is in a low tonal key, while one painted in the pale range of a late Claude Monet is said to be high keyed. The tonal range of pigments is too narrow for the painter to be able to match the brightest lights and deepest darks of nature. Therefore, to express effects of illumination and dense shadow, he must lower the overall tonal key of his design, thus intensifying the brightness value of his lightest pigment colours.

THE NATURE OF COLOUR AND THE LAWS OF COLOUR MIXTURE

Aristotle viewed colour as the product of a mixture of white and black. This was the prevailing belief until 1666, when Isaac Newton's prism experiments provided a scientific basis for the understanding of colour. Newton showed that a prism could break white light into a range of colours, which he called the spectrum. The recombination of these spectral colours remade the white light. Although he recognized that the spectrum was continuous, Newton used the seven colour names red, orange, yellow, green, blue, indigo, and violet for segments of the spectrum by analogy with the seven notes of the musical scale.

The unexpected difference between light perception and sound perception clarifies this curious aspect of colour. When different coloured beams of light, such as red and yellow, are projected onto a white surface in equal amounts, the resulting perception of the eye signals a single colour (in this case, orange) to the brain, a signal that may be identical to that produced by a single beam of light. When, however, if two musical tones are sounded simultaneously, the individual tones can still be easily discerned; the sound produced by a combination of tones is never identical to that

(CONTINUED ON THE NEXT PAGE)

(CONTINUED FROM THE PREVIOUS PAGE)

of a single tone. A tone is the result of a specific sound wave, but a colour can be the result of a single light beam or a combination of any number of light beams.

A colour can, however, be precisely specified by its hue, saturation, and brightness–three attributes sufficient to distinguish it from all other possible perceived colours. The hue is that aspect of colour usually associated with terms such as red, orange, yellow, and so forth. Saturation (also known as chroma or tone) refers to relative purity. When a pure, vivid shade of red is mixed with a variable amount of white, weaker or paler reds are produced, each having the same hue but a different saturation. These paler colours are called unsaturated colours. Finally, light of any given combination of hue and saturation can have a variable brightness (also called intensity or value), which depends on the total amount of light energy present. Newton demonstrated that colour is a quality of light.

Colours of the spectrum are called chromatic colours; there are also nonchromatic colours such as the browns, magentas, and pinks. The term *achromatic colours* is sometimes applied to the black-gray-white sequence. According to some estimates, the eye can distinguish some 10 million colours, all of which derive from two types of light mixture: additive and subtractive. As the names imply, additive mixture involves the addition of spectral components, and subtractive mixture concerns the subtraction or absorption of parts of the spectrum.

Additive mixing occurs when beams of light are combined. The colour circle, first devised by Newton, is still widely used for purposes of colour design and is also useful when the qualitative behavior of mixing beams of light is considered. Newton's colour circle combines the spectral colours red, orange, yellow, green, cyan, indigo, and blue-violet with the nonspectral colour magenta (a mixture of blue-violet and red light beams), as shown in the figure. White is at the centre and is produced by mixing light beams of approximately equal intensities of complementary colours (colours that are diametrically opposed on the colour circle), such as yellow and blue-violet, green and magenta, or cyan and red. Intermediate colours can be produced by mixing light beams, so mixing red and yellow gives orange, mixing red and blue-violet gives magenta, and so on.

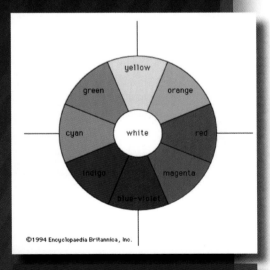

©1994 Encyclopaedia Britannica, Inc.

This example is one form of Isaac Newton's colour circle.

(CONTINUED ON THE NEXT PAGE)

(CONTINUED FROM THE PREVIOUS PAGE)

The three additive primary colours are red, green, and blue; this means that, by additively mixing the colours red, green, and blue in varying amounts, almost all other colours can be produced, and, when the three primaries are added together in equal amounts, white is produced.

Additive mixing can be demonstrated using three slide projectors fitted with filters. One projector shines a beam of saturated red light onto a white screen. Another projector shines a beam of saturated blue light, and the third shines a beam of saturated green light. Additive mixing occurs where the beams overlap (and thus are added together). Where red and green beams overlap, yellow is produced. If more red light is added or if the intensity of the green light is decreased, the light mixture becomes orange. Similarly, if there is more green light than red light, a yellow-green is produced.

Subtractive colour mixing involves the absorption and selective transmission or reflection of light. It occurs when colorants (such as pigments or dyes) are mixed or when several coloured filters are inserted into a single beam of white light. For example, if a projector is fitted with a deep red filter, the filter will transmit red light and absorb other colours. If the projector is fitted with a strong green filter, red light will be absorbed and only green light transmitted. If, therefore, the projector is fitted with

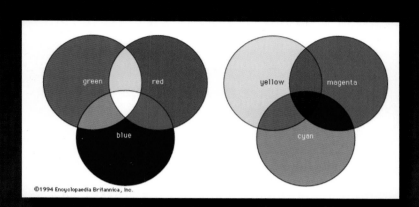

©1994 Encyclopaedia Britannica, Inc.

(*Left*) An illustration shows the additive mixing of primary colours, red, green, and blue. (*Right*) Another depicts the subtractive mixing of magenta, yellow, and cyan.

both red and green filters, all colours will be absorbed and no light transmitted, resulting in black. Similarly, a yellow pigment absorbs blue and violet light while reflecting yellow, green, and red light (the green and red additively combining to produce more yellow). Blue pigment absorbs primarily yellow, orange, and red light. If the yellow and blue pigments are mixed, green will be produced since it is the only spectral component that is not strongly absorbed by either pigment.

Because additive processes have the greatest gamut when the primaries are red, green, and blue, it is reasonable to expect that the greatest gamut in subtractive processes will be achieved when the primaries are, respectively,

(CONTINUED ON THE NEXT PAGE)

(CONTINUED FROM THE PREVIOUS PAGE)

red-absorbing, green-absorbing, and blue-absorbing. The colour of an image that absorbs red light while transmitting all other radiations is blue-green, often called cyan. An image that absorbs only green light transmits both blue light and red light, and its colour is magenta. The blue-absorbing image transmits only green light and red light, and its colour is yellow. Hence, the subtractive primaries are cyan, magenta, and yellow.

No concepts in the field of colour have traditionally been more confused than those just discussed. This confusion can be traced to two prevalent misnomers: the subtractive primary cyan, which is properly a blue-green, is commonly called blue; and the subtractive primary magenta is commonly called red. In these terms, the subtractive primaries become red, yellow, and blue; and those whose experience is confined for the most part to subtractive mixtures have good cause to wonder why the physicist insists on regarding red, green, and blue as the primary colours. The confusion is at once resolved when it is realized that red, green, and blue are selected as additive primaries because they provide the greatest colour gamut in mixtures. For the same reason, the subtractive primaries are, respectively, red-absorbing (cyan), green-absorbing (magenta), and blue-absorbing (yellow).

The Greco-Roman, Renaissance, and Neoclassical method of representing volume and space in painting was by a system of notated tonal values, the direction of each plane in the design being indicated by a particular degree of lightness or darkness. Each tonal value was determined by the angle at which a plane was meant to appear to turn away from an imaginary light source. The tonal modeling, or shading, of forms was often first completed in a monochrome underpainting. This was then coloured with transparent washes of local hues, a technique similar to that of colour tinting a black-and-white photograph.

Each hue has an intrinsic tonal value in relation to others on the chromatic scale; orange is inherently lighter than red, for instance, and violet is darker than green. Any reversal of this natural tonal order creates a colour discord. An optical shock is therefore produced when orange is juxtaposed with pink (a lighter tone of red) or pale violet is placed against dark green. Such contrasts as these may be deliberately used in paintings to achieve a dramatic and disturbing effect.

The intensity of a colour is its degree of purity or hue saturation. The colour of a geranium, therefore, is said to be more intense, more highly saturated with pure orange-red than is mahogany. The pigment vermilion is orange-red at maximum intensity; the brown earth

This detail is an example of the early oil method of (*left*) colour glazing a (*right*) monochrome painting.

pigment burnt sienna is grayer and has a lower degree of orange-red saturation.

Intense hues are called chromatic colours. The achromatic range is made up of hues reduced in intensity by the addition of white, making the tints, or pastel colours, such as cream and pink; or of black, producing the shades, or earth colours, such as mustard and moss green; or of both white and black, creating the neutralized hues, or colour-tinged grays, such as oatmeal and charcoal.

An achromatic colour will seem more intense if it is surrounded by neutralized hues or juxtaposed with its complementary colour. Complementaries are colour opposites. The complementary colour to one of the primary hues is the mixture of the other two. The complementary to red pigment, for example, is green— that is, blue mixed with yellow. The colour wheel shows that the tertiaries also have their colour opposites, the complementary to orange-red, for instance, being blue-green. Under clear light the complementary to any chroma, shade, or tint can be seen if one "fixates," or stares at, one colour intently for a few seconds then looks at a neutral, preferably white, surface. The colour afterimage will appear to glow on the neutral surface. Mutual enhancement of colour intensity results from juxtaposing a complementary pair, red becoming more intensely red, for instance, and green more fiercely green when these are contiguous than either would appear if surrounded by harmonious hues. The 19th-century physicist Michel-Eugène Chevreul referred to this mutual exaltation of opposites as the law of simultaneous contrast. Chevreul's second law, of successive contrast, referred to the optical sensation that a complementary colour halo appears gradually to surround an intense hue. This complementary glow is superimposed on surrounding weaker colours, a gray becoming greenish when juxtaposed with red, reddish in close relationship with green, yellowish against violet, and so on.

Hues containing a high proportion of blue (the violet to green range) appear cooler than those with a high content of yellow or red (the green-yellow to red-violet range). This difference in the temperature of hues in a particular painting is, of course, relative to the range and juxtaposition of colours in the design. A green will appear cool if surrounded by intense yellow, while it will seem warm against blue-green. The optical tendency for warm colours to advance before cold had been long exploited by European and Asian painters as a method of suggesting spatial depth. Changes in temperature and intensity can be observed in the atmospheric effects of nature, where the colours of distant forms become cooler, grayer, and bluish, while foreground planes and features appear more intense and usually warmer in colour.

The apparent changes in a hue as it

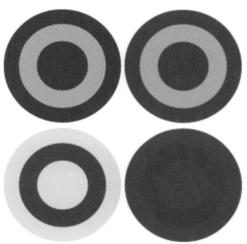

©1995 Encyclopaedia Britannica, Inc.

(*Top*) By complementary action, the same gray pigment will appear greenish when adjacent to red but reddish if adjacent to green. (*Bottom*) A green hue will seem cool if surrounded by yellow but warm when surrounded by blue-green.

passes through zones of different colour has enabled painters in many periods to create the illusion of having employed a wide range of pigment hues with, in fact, the use of very few. And, although painters had applied many of the optical principles of colour behavior intuitively in the past, the publication of research findings by Chevreul and others stimulated the Neo-Impressionists and Post-Impressionists and the later Orphist and Op art painters to extend systematically the expressive possibilities of these principles in order to create illusions of volume and space and vibrating sensations of light and movement. Paul Cézanne, for example, demonstrated that subtle changes in the surface of a form and in its spatial relationship to others could be expressed primarily in facets of colour, modulated by varying degrees of tone, intensity, and temperature and by the introduction of complementary colour accents.

While the often complex religious and cultural colour symbologies may be understood by very few, the emotional response to certain colour combinations appears to be almost universal. Optical harmonies and discords seem to affect everyone in the same way, if in varying degrees. Thus, an image repeated in different schemes of colour will express a different mood in each change.

TEXTURE

Pointillism (a term given to the Neo-Impressionist system of representing the shimmer of atmospheric light with spots of coloured pigment) produced an overall granular texture. As an element of design,

In his *Study for A Sunday on La Grande Jatte* (1884), Georges Seurat used small, dot-like dabs of contrasting colours to create a painting that would blend together in a viewer's eyes. The style was called Pointillism.

texture includes all areas of a painting enriched or animated by vibrating patterns of lines, shapes, tones, and colours, in addition to the tactile textures created by the plastic qualities of certain mediums. Decorative textures may be of geometrical repeat patterns, as in much of Indian, Islamic, and medieval European painting and other art, or of representations of patterns in nature, such as scattered leaves, falling snow, and flights of birds.

GEORGES SEURAT

The French painter Georges Seurat (1859–1891) was the founder of the 19th-century French school of Neo-Impressionism whose technique for portraying the play of light using tiny brushstrokes of contrasting colours became known as Pointillism. Using this technique, he created huge compositions with tiny, detached strokes of pure colour too small to be distinguished when looking at the entire work but making his paintings shimmer with brilliance. Works in this style include *Une Baignade, Asnières* (1883–84) and *A Sunday on La Grande Jatte–1884* (1884–86).

While attending school, Seurat began to draw, and, beginning in 1875, he took a course from a sculptor, Justin Lequien. He officially entered the École des Beaux-Arts in 1878, in the class of Henri Lehmann, a disciple of Ingres, who painted portraits and conventional nudes. In the school library Seurat discovered a book that was to inspire him for the rest of his life: the *Essai sur les signes inconditionnels de l'art* (1827; "Essay on the Unmistakable Signs of Art"), by Humbert de Superville, a painter-engraver from Geneva; it dealt with the future course of aesthetics and with the relationship between lines and images. Seurat was also impressed with the work of another Genevan aesthetician, David Sutter, who combined mathematics and musicology. Throughout his brief career, Seurat manifested an unusually strong interest in the intellectual and scientific bases of art.

In November 1879, at the age of 20, Seurat went to Brest to do his military service. There he drew the sea, beaches, and boats. When he returned to Paris the following autumn, he shared a studio with another painter, Édmond-François Aman-Jean, who then joined him in Lehmann's class. But Seurat and Aman-Jean departed from the policies of the École des Beaux-Arts in admiring the warm landscapes of Jean-Baptiste Millet at the Louvre. The two friends often frequented dance halls and cabarets in the evening, and in spring they took the passenger steamer to the island of La Grande Jatte, the setting of Seurat's future paintings. Seurat exhibited at the official Salon–the state-sponsored annual exhibition–for the first time in 1883. He displayed portraits of his mother and of his friend Aman-Jean, and in that same year he began his studies, sketches, and panels for *Une Baignade, Asnières*. When the picture was refused by the jury of the Salon in 1884, Seurat decided to participate in the foundation of the Groupe des

(CONTINUED ON THE NEXT PAGE)

(CONTINUED FROM THE PREVIOUS PAGE)

Artistes Indépendants, an association "with neither jury nor prizes," where he showed his *Baignade* in June.

During this period, he had seen and been strongly influenced by the monumental symbolic paintings of Puvis de Chavannes. He also met the 100-year-old chemist Michel-Eugène Chevreul and experimented with Chevreul's theories of the chromatic circle of light and studied the effects that could be achieved with the three primary colours (yellow, red, and blue) and their complements. Seurat fell in with Paul Signac, who was to become his chief disciple, and painted many rough sketches on small boards in preparation for his masterpiece, *A Sunday on La Grande Jatte–1884*. In December 1884 he exhibited the *Baignade* again, with the Société des Artistes Indépendents, which was to be of immense influence in the development of modern art.

Seurat spent the winter of 1885 working on the island of La Grande Jatte and the summer at Grandcamp, in Normandy. The Impressionist master Camille Pissarro, who was temporarily converted to the technique of Pointillism, was introduced to Seurat by Signac during this period. Seurat finished the painting *La Grande Jatte* and exhibited it from May 15 to June 15, 1886, at an Impressionist group show.

This picture demonstration of his technique aroused great interest. Seurat's chief artistic associates at this time, painters also concerned with the effects of light on colour, were Signac and Pissarro. The unexpectedness of his art and the novelty of his conception excited the Belgian poet Émile Verhaeren. The critic Félix Fénéon praised Seurat's method in an avant-garde review. And Seurat's work was exhibited by the eminent dealer Durand-Ruel in Paris and in New York City.

In 1887, while he was temporarily living in a garret studio, Seurat began work on *Les Poseuses*. This painting was to be the last of his compositions on the grand scale of the *Baignade* and *La Grande Jatte*; he thought about adding a Place Clichy to this number but abandoned the idea. In the following year he completed *Les Poseuses* and also *La Parade*. In February 1888 he went to Brussels with Signac for a private viewing of the exposition of the Twenty (XX), a small group of independent artists, in which he showed seven canvases, including *La Grande Jatte*.

Seurat participated in the 1889 Salon des Indépendants, exhibiting landscapes. He painted Signac's portrait at this time. His residence at this point was in the Pigalle district, where he lived with his 21-year-old mistress, Madeleine Knobloch. On February 16, 1890,

(CONTINUED ON THE NEXT PAGE)

(CONTINUED FROM THE PREVIOUS PAGE)

Madeleine presented him with a son, whom he officially acknowledged and entered in the register of births under the name of Pierre-Georges Seurat. During that year Seurat completed the painting *Le Chahut*, which he sent to the exhibition of the Twenty (XX) in Brussels. During that period he also painted the *Jeune Femme se poudrant*, a portrait of his mistress, though he continued to conceal his liaison with her even from his most intimate friends. He spent that summer at Gravelines, near Dunkirk, where he painted several landscapes and planned what was to be his last painting, *Le Cirque*.

As if from some sort of premonition of his impending death, Seurat showed the uncompleted *Cirque* at the eighth Salon des Indépendants. As an organizer of the exhibition, he exhausted himself in the presentation and hanging of the works. He caught a chill, developed infectious angina, and, before the exhibition was ended, he died on Easter Sunday 1891. Seurat was buried in the family vault at Père Lachaise cemetery. In addition to his seven monumental paintings, he left 40 smaller paintings and sketches, about 500 drawings, and several sketchbooks. Though a modest output in terms of quantity, they show him to have been among the foremost painters of one of the greatest periods in the history of art.

VOLUME AND SPACE

The perceptual and conceptual methods of representing volume and space on the flat surface of a painting are related to the two levels of understanding spatial relationships in everyday life.

Perceptual space is the view of things at a particular time and from a fixed position. This is the stationary window view recorded by the camera and represented in the later periods of ancient Greek and Roman paintings and in most Western schools of painting since the Renaissance. Illusions of perceptual space are generally created by use of the linear perspectival system, based on the observations that objects appear to the eye to shrink and parallel lines and planes to converge as they approach the horizon, or viewer's eye level.

Young children and untrained artists, however, do not understand space in this way and represent it conceptually. Their paintings, therefore, show objects and surroundings independently of one another and from the views that best present their most characteristic features. The notion of scale in their pictures is also subjective, the relative size of things being decided by the artist either by their degree of emotional significance for him or by their narrative importance in the picture (interest perspective).

The conceptual, polydimensional representation of space has been used at some period in most cultures. In much of ancient Egyptian and Cretan painting, for example, the head and legs of a figure were shown in profile, but the eye and torso were drawn frontally. And in Indian, Islamic, and pre-Renaissance European painting, vertical forms and surfaces were represented by their most informative elevation view (as if seen from

LINEAR AND AERIAL PERSPECTIVE AND ANAMORPHOSIS

Perspective is the method of graphically depicting three-dimensional objects and spatial relationships on a two-dimensional plane or on a plane that is shallower than the original.

Linear perspective is a system of creating an illusion of depth on a flat surface. All parallel lines (orthogonals) in a painting or drawing using this system converge in a single vanishing point on the composition's horizon line.

Linear perspective is thought to have been devised about 1415 by Italian Renaissance architect Filippo Brunelleschi and later documented by architect and writer Leon Battista Alberti in 1435 (*Della Pittura*). Linear perspective was likely evident to artists and architects in the ancient Greek and Roman periods, but no records exist from that time, and the practice was thus lost until the 15th century.

The three components essential to the linear perspective system are orthogonals, the horizon line, and a vanishing point. So as to appear farther from the viewer, objects in the compositions are rendered increasingly smaller as they near the vanishing point. Early examples of Brunelleschi's system can be seen in Donatello's relief *St. George Killing the Dragon* (c. 1416–17) and Masaccio's painting

The Holy Trinity (1425–27), a dramatic illusion- istic crucifixion. Andrea Mantegna (who also mastered the technique of foreshortening), Leonardo da Vinci, and German artist Albrecht Dürer are considered some of the early mas- ters of linear perspective. As the limitations of linear perspective became apparent, artists invented additional devices (e.g., foreshort- ening and anamorphosis) to achieve the most-convincing illusion of space and distance.

Aerial perspective, also called atmospheric perspective, is a method of creating the illusion of depth, or recession, in a painting or draw- ing by modulating colour to simulate changes effected by the atmosphere on the colours of things seen at a distance. Although the use of aerial perspective has been known since antiquity, Leonardo da Vinci first used the term aerial perspective in his *Treatise on Painting*, in which he wrote: "Colours become weaker in proportion to their distance from the person who is looking at them." It was later discov- ered that the presence in the atmosphere of moisture and of tiny particles of dust and simi- lar material causes a scattering of light as it passes through them, the degree of scattering being dependent on the wavelength, which cor- responds to the colour, of the light. Because light of short wavelength–blue light–is scat- tered most, the colours of all distant dark objects tend toward blue; for example, distant

(CONTINUED ON THE NEXT PAGE)

(*CONTINUED FROM THE PREVIOUS PAGE*)

mountains have a bluish cast. Light of long wavelength—red light—is scattered least; thus, distant bright objects appear redder because some of the blue is scattered and lost from the light by which they are seen.

The intervening atmosphere between a viewer and, for example, distant mountains, creates other visual effects that can be mimicked by landscape painters. The atmosphere causes distant forms to have less distinct edges and outlines than forms near the viewer, and interior detail is similarly softened or blurred. Distant objects appear somewhat lighter than objects of similar tone lying closer at hand, and in general contrasts between light and shade appear less extreme at great distances. All these effects are more apparent at the base of a mountain than at its peak, since the density of the intervening atmosphere is greater at lower elevations.

Examples of aerial perspective have been found in ancient Greco-Roman wall paintings. The techniques were lost from European art during the "Dark" and Middle Ages and were rediscovered by Flemish painters of the 15th century (such as Joachim Patinir), after which they became a standard element in the European painter's technical vocabulary. The 19th-century British landscape painter J.M.W. Turner made perhaps the boldest and most ambitious use of aerial perspective among Western artists. Aerial perspective was used with great sophistication and pictorial effectiveness by Chinese landscape painters from about the 8th century on.

Anamorphosis is an ingenious perspective technique that gives a distorted image of the subject represented in a picture when seen from the usual viewpoint but so executed that if viewed from a particular angle, or reflected in a curved mirror, the distortion disappears and the image in the picture appears normal. Derived from the Greek word meaning "to transform," the term *anamorphosis* was first employed in the 17th century, although this technique had been one of the more curious by-products of the discovery of perspective in the 14th and 15th centuries.

The first examples of the technique appear in Leonardo da Vinci's notebooks. It was regarded as a display of technical virtuosity, and it was included in most 16th- and 17th-century drawing manuals. Two important examples of anamorphosis are a portrait of Edward VI (1546) that has been attributed to William Scrots, and a skull in the foreground of Hans Holbein the Younger's painting of Jean de Dinteville and Georges de Selve, *The Ambassadors* (1533). Many examples are provided with special peepholes through which

(CONTINUED ON THE NEXT PAGE)

(CONTINUED FROM THE PREVIOUS PAGE)

can be seen the rectified view that first eluded the viewer.

A modern equivalent of anamorphosis is the so-called Ames Room, in which people and objects are distorted by manipulation of the contours of the room in which they are seen. This and other aspects of anamorphosis received a good deal of attention in the 20th century from psychologists interested in perception.

Artists and architects in the 21st century continued to experiment with anamorphic designs. In 2014 Swiss artist Felice Varini—known for large-scale anamorphic installations—created *Three Ellipses for Three Locks*, for which he painted three ellipses, segments of which covered roads, walls, and nearly 100 buildings in the historic centre of the city of Hasselt, Belgium. The design became coherent only when viewed from a particular vantage point in the city.

ground level), while the horizontal planes on which they stood were shown in isometric plan (as if viewed from above). This system produces the overall effect that objects and their surroundings have been compressed within a shallow space behind the picture plane.

By the end of the 19th century Cézanne had flattened the conventional Renaissance picture space, tilting horizontal planes so that they appeared to push vertical forms and surfaces forward from the picture plane and toward the spectator. This illusion of the picture surface as an integrated structure in project- ing low relief was developed further in the early 20th century by the Cubists. The conceptual, rotary perspec- tive of a Cubist painting shows not only the components of things from different viewpoints but presents every plane of an object and its immediate surroundings simultaneously. This gives the composite impression of things in space that is gained by having examined their surfaces and construction from every angle.

In modern painting, both conceptual and perceptual methods of representing space are often combined. And, where the orbital movement of forms—which has been a basic element in European design since the Renaissance—was intended to hold the spectator's attention within the frame, the expanding picture space in late 20th- and early 21st-century mural-size abstract paintings directs the eye outward to the surrounding wall, and their shapes and colours seem about to invade the observer's own territory.

TIME AND MOVEMENT

Time and movement in painting are not restricted to representations of physical energy, but they are ele- ments of all design. Part of the viewer's full experience of a great painting is to allow the arrangement of lines, shapes, and accents of tone or colour to guide the eye across the picture surface at controlled tempos and rhythmic directions. These arrangements contribute overall to the expression of a particular mood, vision, and idea.

Centuries before cinematography, painters attempted to produce kinetic sensations on a flat surface. A mural of 2000 BCE in an Egyptian tomb at Beni Hasan, for instance, is designed as a continuous strip sequence of wrestling holds and throws, so accurately articulated and notated that it might be photographed as an animated film cartoon. The gradual unrolling of a 12th-century Japanese hand scroll produces the visual sensation of a helicopter flight along a river valley, while the experience of walking to the end of a long, processional Renaissance mural by Andrea Mantegna or Benozzo Gozzoli is similar to that of having witnessed a passing pageant as a standing spectator.

In the Eastern and Western narrative convention of continuous representation, various incidents in a story were depicted together within one design, the chief characters in the drama easily identified as they reappeared in different situations and settings throughout the painting. In Byzantine murals and in Indian and medieval manuscript paintings, narrative sequences were depicted in grid patterns, each "compartment" of the design representing a visual chapter in a religious story or a mythological or historical epic.

The Cubists aimed to give the viewer the time experience of moving around static forms in order to examine their volume and structure and their relationships to the space surrounding them. In paintings such as *Nude Descending a Staircase*, *Girl Running on a Balcony*, and *Dog on Leash*, Marcel Duchamp and Giacomo Balla combined the Cubist technique of projected, interlocking planes with the superimposed time-motion sequences of cinematography. This technique enabled the artists to analyze the structural mechanics of forms, which are represented as moving in space past the viewer.

GIACOMO BALLA

Italian artist Giacomo Balla (1871–1958) was a founding member of the Futurist movement in painting.

Balla had little formal art training, having attended briefly an academy in Turin. He moved to Rome in his twenties. As a young artist, he was greatly influenced by French Neo-Impressionism during a sojourn he made in Paris in 1900. Upon his return to Rome, he adopted the Neo-Impressionist style and imparted it to two younger artists, Umberto Boccioni and Gino Severini. Balla's early works reflect contemporary French trends but also hint at his lifelong interest in rendering light and its effects. Balla, Boccioni, and Severini gradually came under the influence of the Milanese poet Filippo Marinetti, who in 1909 launched the literary movement he called Futurism, which was an attempt to revitalize Italian culture by embracing the power of modern science and technology. In 1910 Balla and other Italian artists published the "Technical Manifesto of Futurist Painting."

Unlike most Futurists, Balla was a lyrical painter, unconcerned with modern machines or violence. *The Street Light—Study of Light*

(CONTINUED ON THE NEXT PAGE)

(*CONTINUED FROM THE PREVIOUS PAGE*)

(1909), for example, is a dynamic depiction of light. Despite his unique taste in subject matter, in works such as this Balla conveys a sense of speed and urgency that puts his paintings in line with Futurism's fascination with the energy of modern life. One of his best-known works, *Dynamism of a Dog on a Leash* (1912), shows an almost frame-by-frame view of a woman walking a dog on a boulevard. The work illustrates his principle of simultaneity—i.e., the rendering of motion by simultaneously showing many aspects of a moving object. This interest in capturing a single moment in a series of planes was derived from Cubism, but it was also no doubt tied to Balla's interest in the technology of photography.

During World War I Balla composed a series of paintings in which he attempted to convey the impression of movement or velocity through the use of planes of colour; these works are perhaps the most abstract of all Futurist paintings. After the war he remained faithful to the Futurist style long after its other practitioners had abandoned it. In addition to his painting, during these years he explored stage design, graphic design, and even acting. At the end of his career he abandoned his lifelong pursuit of near abstraction and reverted to a more traditional style.

DESIGN PRINCIPLES

Because painting is a two-dimensional art, the flat pattern of lines and shapes is an important aspect of design, even for those painters concerned with creating illusions of great depth. And, since any mark made on the painting surface can be perceived as a spatial statement—for it rests upon it—there are also qualities of three-dimensional design in paintings composed primarily of flat shapes. Shapes in a painting, therefore, may be balanced with one another as units of a flat pattern and considered at the same time as components in a spatial design, balanced one behind another. A symmetrical balance of tone and colour masses of equal weight creates a serene and sometimes monumental design, while a more dynamic effect is created by an asymmetrical balance.

Geometrical shapes and masses are often the basic units in the design of both "flat patterns," such as Byzantine and Islamic paintings, and "sculptural compositions," such as Baroque and Neoclassical figure tableaux. The flat, overlapping squares, circles, and triangles that create the pattern of a Romanesque mural, for example, become the interlocking cubic, spherical, and pyramidal components that enclose the grouped figures and surrounding features in a Renaissance or a Neoclassical composition.

An emphasis upon the proportion of the parts to the whole is a characteristic of Classical styles of painting. The Golden Mean, or Section, has been used as an ideal proportion on which to base the framework of lines and shapes in the design of a painting. The Renaissance mathematician Lucas Pacioli defined this aesthetically satisfying ratio as the division of a line so that the shorter part is to the longer as the longer is to the whole

GOLDEN MEAN

The Golden Mean is also known as the golden section, golden ratio, or divine proportion. In mathematics, it is the irrational number $(1 + \sqrt{5})/2$, often denoted by the Greek letters τ or ϕ, and approximately equal to 1.618. The origin of this number and its name may be traced back to about 500 BCE and the investigation in Pythagorean geometry of the regular pentagon, in which the five diagonals form a five-pointed star. On each such diagonal lie two points of intersection with other diagonals, and either of those points divides the whole diagonal into two segments of unequal lengths so that the ratio of the whole diagonal to the larger segment equals the ratio of the larger segment to the smaller one. In terms of present day algebra, letting the length of the shorter segment be one unit and the length of the larger segment be x units gives rise to the equation $(x + 1)/x = x/1$; this may be rearranged to form the quadratic equation $x^2 - x - 1 = 0$, for which the positive solution is $x = (1 + \sqrt{5})/2$, the golden ratio.

The ancient Greeks recognized this "dividing" or "sectioning" property and described it generally as "the division of a line into

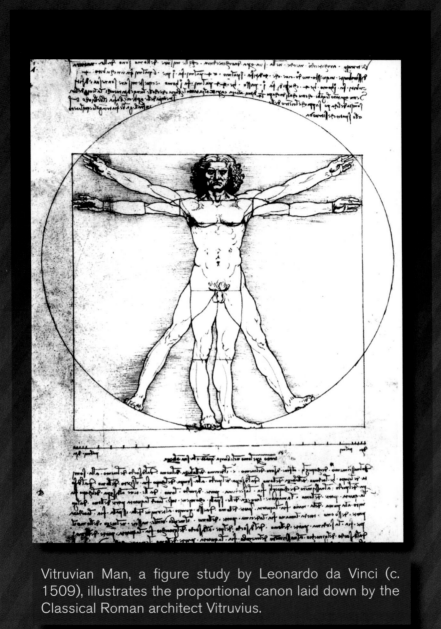

Vitruvian Man, a figure study by Leonardo da Vinci (c. 1509), illustrates the proportional canon laid down by the Classical Roman architect Vitruvius.

(CONTINUED ON THE NEXT PAGE)

(*CONTINUED FROM THE PREVIOUS PAGE*)

extreme and mean ratio," a phrase that was ultimately shortened to simply "the section." It was more than 2,000 years later that both "ratio" and "section" were designated as "golden" in references by the German astronomer Johannes Kepler and others. The Greeks also had observed that the golden ratio provided the most aesthetically pleasing proportion of sides of a rectangle, a notion that was enhanced during the Renaissance by, for example, work of the Italian polymath Leonardo da Vinci and the publication of *De divina proportione* (1509; *Divine Proportion*) by the Italian mathematician Luca Pacioli, and illustrated by Leonardo.

The golden ratio occurs in many mathematical contexts. It is geometrically constructible by straightedge and compass, and it occurs in the investigation of the Archimedean and Platonic solids. It is the limit of the ratios of consecutive terms of the Fibonacci number sequence 1, 1, 2, 3, 5, 8, 13, ..., in which each term beyond the second is the sum of the previous two, and it is also the value of the most basic of continued fractions, namely $1 + 1/(1 + 1/(1 + 1/(1 + ...$

In modern mathematics, the golden ratio occurs in the description of fractals, figures that exhibit self-similarity and play an important role in the study of chaos and dynamical systems.

(approximately 8 to 13). His treatise (*Divina proportione*) influenced Leonardo da Vinci and Albrecht Dürer. The Neo-Impressionists Georges Seurat and Paul Signac based the linear pattern of many of their compositions upon the principle of this "divine proportion." Golden Mean proportions can be discovered in the design of many other styles of painting, although often they may have been created more by intuitive judgment than by calculated measurement.

Tension is created in paintings, as it is experienced in everyday life, by the anticipation of an event or by an unexpected change in the order of things. Optical and psychological tensions occur in passages of a design, therefore, when lines or shapes almost touch or seem about to collide, when a harmonious colour progression is interrupted by a sudden discord, or when an asymmetrical balance of lines, shapes, tones, or colours is barely held.

Contrasts in line, shape, tone, and colour create vitality; rectilinear shapes played against curvilinear, for instance, or warm colours against cool. Or a painting may be composed in contrasted overall patterns, superimposed in counterpoint to one another—a colour scheme laid across contrasting patterns of lines and tones, for example.

DESIGN RELATIONSHIPS WITH PAINTING AND OTHER VISUAL ARTS

The philosophy and spirit of a particular period in painting usually have been reflected in many of its other visual arts. The ideas and aspirations of the ancient cultures, of the Renaissance, Baroque, Rococo, and Neoclassical periods of Western art and, more recently, of the 19th-century Art Nouveau and Secessionist movements were expressed in much of the architecture, interior design, furniture, textiles, ceramics, dress design, and handicrafts, as well as in the fine arts, of their times. Following the Industrial Revolution, with the redundancy of handcraftsmanship and the loss of direct communication between the fine artist and society, idealistic efforts to unite the arts and crafts in service to the community were made by William Morris in Victorian England and by the Bauhaus in 20th-century Germany. Although their aims were not fully realized, their influences, like those of the short-lived de Stijl and Constructivist movements, have been far-reaching, particularly in architectural, furniture, and typographic design.

Michelangelo and Leonardo da Vinci were painters, sculptors, and architects. Although no artists since have excelled in so wide a range of creative design, leading 20th-century painters expressed their ideas in many other mediums. In graphic design, for example, Pierre Bonnard, Henri Matisse, and Raoul Dufy produced posters and illustrated books; André Derain, Fernand Léger, Marc Chagall, Mikhail Larionov, Robert Rauschenberg, and David Hockney designed for the theatre; Joan Miró, Pablo Picasso, and Chagall worked in ceramics; Georges Braque and Salvador Dalí designed jewelry; and Dalí, Hans Richter, and Andy Warhol made films. Many of them, with other modern painters, have also been sculptors and printmakers and have designed for textiles, tapestries, mosaics, and stained glass, while there are few mediums of the visual arts that Picasso did not work in and revitalize.

In turn, painters have been stimulated by the imagery, techniques, and design of other visual arts. One of the earliest of these influences was possibly from the theatre, where the ancient Greeks are thought to have been the first to employ the illusions of optical perspective. The discovery or reappraisal of design techniques and imagery in the art forms and processes of other cultures has been an important stimulus to the development of more recent styles of Western painting, whether or not their traditional significance have been fully understood. The influence of Japanese woodcut prints on Synthetism and the Nabis, for example, and of African sculpture on Cubism and the German Expressionists helped to create visual vocabularies and syntax with which to express new visions and ideas. The invention of photography introduced painters to new aspects of nature, while eventually prompting others to abandon representational painting altogether. Painters of everyday life, such as Edgar Degas, Henri de Toulouse-Lautrec, Édouard Vuillard, and Bonnard, exploited the design innovations of camera cutoffs, close-ups, and unconventional viewpoints in order to give the spectator the sensation of sharing an intimate picture space with the figures and objects in the painting.

PROCEDURES AND MEDIUMS

Whether a painting reached completion by careful stages or was executed directly by a hit-or-miss alla prima method (in which pigments are laid on in a single application) was once largely determined by the ideals and established techniques of its cultural tradition. For example, the medieval European illuminator's painstaking procedure, by which a complex linear pattern was gradually enriched with gold leaf and precious pigments, was contemporary with the Song Chinese Chan (Zen) practice of immediate, calligraphic brush painting, following a contemplative period of spiritual self-preparation. More recently, the artist has decided the technique and working method best suited to his aims and temperament. In France in the 1880s, for instance, Seurat might be working in his studio on drawings, tone studies, and colour schemes in preparation for a large composition at the same time that, outdoors, Monet was endeavouring to capture the effects of afternoon light and atmosphere, while Cézanne analyzed the structure of the mountain Sainte-Victoire with deliberated brush strokes, laid as irrevocably as mosaic tesserae (small pieces, such as marble or tile).

Claude Monet painted *Stacks of Wheat (Sunset, Snow Effect)* (1890–91) outdoors to capture the fleeting effects of light. The practice of painting landscapes in the open air is called plein-air painting.

WORKING PROCEDURE

The kind of relationship established between artist and patron, the site and subject matter of a painting commission, and the physical properties of the medium employed may also dictate working procedure. Peter Paul Rubens, for example, followed the businesslike 17th-century custom of submitting a small oil sketch, or *modella*, for his client's approval before carrying out a large-scale commission. Siting problems peculiar to mural painting, such as spectator eye level and the scale, style, and function of a building interior, had first to be solved in preparatory drawings and sometimes with the use of wax figurines or scale models

CANVAS AND SIZING

Canvas is a stout cloth probably named after *cannabis* (Latin: "hemp"). Hemp and flax fibre have been used for ages to produce cloth for sails. Certain classes are termed sailcloth or canvas synonymously. After the introduction of the power loom, canvas was made from flax, hemp, tow, jute, cotton, and mixtures of such fibres. Flax canvas is essentially of double warp, for it is invariably intended to withstand pressure or rough usage.

Canvas yarns (usually cotton, flax, or jute) are almost invariably two or more ply, an arrangement that tends to produce a uniform thickness. A plain weave is extensively used for these fabrics, but in many cases special weaves are used that leave the open spaces well defined.

Artists' canvas, a single-warp variety, used for painting in oils, is much lighter than sail canvas. The best qualities are made of cream or bleached flax fibre about 25 cm (10 inches) long (line). An admixture of shorter linen fibre (tow), and even of cotton is found in the commoner kinds. When the cloth comes from the loom it is treated to prepare the surface for the paint.

Sizing is the process of coating a gelatinous or other substance to add strength or stiffness or to reduce absorbency to a canvas. The canvas is prepared for painting by applying size, the dilute mixture of glue or resinous substance. In oil painting it is essential that the canvas be coated with size so that its absorbency is reduced and contact with the paint, which would lead ultimately to the decay of the canvas fibre, is avoided. Hide glue is most frequently used to treat canvas, having largely replaced parchment size, which was recommended by the 14th-century Italian artist and writer Cennino Cennini. (Cennini is best known for writing *Il libro dell'arte* [1437; *The Craftsman's Handbook*], the most informative source on the methods, techniques, and attitudes of medieval artists.)

Tsuguharu Foujita sizes a canvas in 1931. A size such as glue, flour, varnish, or resin can be used to fill pores in a surface or to coat a canvas to decrease the absorption of paints.

of the interior. Scale working drawings are essential to the speed and precision of execution demanded by quick-drying mediums, such as *buon'* ("true") fresco on wet plaster and acrylic resin on canvas. The drawings traditionally are covered with a network of squares, or "squared-up," for enlarging on the surface of the support. Some modern painters prefer to outline the enlargement of a sketch projected directly onto the support by epidiascope (a projector for images of both opaque and transparent objects).

In Renaissance painters' workshops, pupil assistants not only ground and mixed the pigments and prepared the supports and painting surfaces but often laid in the outlines and broad masses of the painting from the master's design and studies.

This Renaissance cassone (plural: cassoni), painted and gilded wood, is from 15th-century Florence. Cassoni were traditionally used as a marriage chest to contain a bride's clothes and dowry.

PRESERVATIVES

The inherent properties of its medium or the atmospheric conditions of its site may themselves preserve
a painting. The wax solvent binder of encaustic paintings both retains the intensity and tonality of the original
colours and protects the surface from damp. And,
while prehistoric rock paintings and *buon'* frescoes
are preserved by natural chemical action, the tempera
pigments thought to be bound only with water on
many ancient Egyptian murals are protected by the dry
atmosphere and unvarying temperature of the tombs. It
has, however, been customary to varnish oil paintings,
both to protect the surface against damage by dirt and
handling and to restore the tonality lost when some
darker pigments dry out into a higher key. Unfortunately,
varnish tends to darken and yellow with time into the
sometimes disastrously imitated "Old Masters' mellow
patina." Once cherished, this amber-gravy film is now
generally removed to reveal the colours in their original
intensity. Glass began to replace varnish toward the end
of the 19th century, when painters wished to retain the
fresh, luminous finish of pigments applied directly to a
pure white ground. The air-conditioning and tempera-
ture-control systems of modern museums make both
varnishing and glazing unnecessary, except for older
and more fragile exhibits.

The frames surrounding early altarpieces, icons, and
cassone panels (painted panels on the chest used for
a bride's household linen) were often structural parts
of the support. With the introduction of portable easel
pictures, heavy frames not only provided some protection against theft and damage but were considered an

aesthetic enhancement to a painting, and frame making became a specialized craft. Gilded gesso moldings (consisting of plaster of paris and sizing that forms the surface for low relief) in extravagant swags of fruit and flowers certainly seem almost an extension of the restless, exuberant design of a Baroque or Rococo painting. A substantial frame also provided a proscenium (in a theatre, the area between the orchestra and the curtain) in which the picture was isolated from its immediate surroundings, thus adding to the window view illusion intended by the artist. Deep, ornate frames are unsuitable for many modern paintings, where the artist's intention is for his forms to appear to advance toward the spectator rather than be viewed by him as if through a wall aperture. In contemporary Minimal paintings, no effects of spatial illusionism are intended; and, in order to emphasize the physical shape of the support itself and to stress its flatness, these abstract, geometrical designs are displayed without frames or are merely edged with thin protective strips of wood or metal.

MEDIUMS

By technical definition, mediums are the liquids added to paints to bind them and make them workable. They are discussed here, however, in the wider meaning of all the various paints, tools, supports, surfaces, and techniques employed by painters. The basis of all paints is variously coloured pigment, ground to a fine powder. The different expressive capacities and characteristic final surface texture of each medium are determined by the vehicle with which it is bound and thinned, the nature and surface preparation of the support, and the tools and technique with which it is handled.

Pigments are derived from various natural and artificial sources. The oldest and most permanent pigments are the blacks, prepared from bone and charcoal, and the clay earths, such as raw umber and raw sienna, which can be changed by heating into darker, warmer browns. In early periods of painting, readily available pigments were few. Certain intense hues were obtainable only from the rarer minerals, such as cinnabar (orange-red vermilion), lapis lazuli (violet-blue ultramarine), and malachite (green). These were expensive and therefore reserved for focal accents and important symbolic features in the design. The opening of trade routes and the manufacture of synthetic substitutes gradually extended the range of colours available to painters.

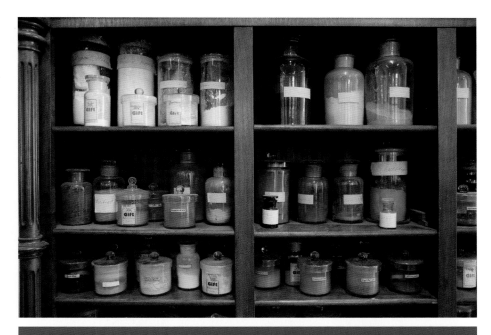

These old pigments are from a restoration studio in Berlin, Germany, that was used to restore two paintings by the Italian Renaissance artist Sandro Botticelli (1445–1510).

PIGMENTS

Pigments are any of a group of compounds that are intensely coloured and are used to colour other materials.

Pigments are insoluble and are applied not as solutions but as finely ground solid particles mixed with a liquid. In general, the same pigments are employed in oil- and water-based paints, printing inks, and plastics. Pigments may be organic (i.e., contain carbon) or inorganic. The majority of inorganic pigments are brighter and last longer than organic ones. Organic pigments made from natural sources have been used for centuries, but most pigments used today are either inorganic or synthetic organic ones. Synthetic organic pigments are derived from coal tars and other petrochemicals. Inorganic pigments are made by relatively simple chemical reactions, notably oxidation, or are found naturally as earths.

Inorganic pigments include white opaque pigments used to provide opacity and to lighten other colours. The most important member of the class is titanium dioxide. White extender pigments are added to paints to lower their cost or improve their properties.

This class includes calcium carbonate, calcium sulfate, diatomaceous silica (the remains of marine organisms), and china clays. Black pigments are primarily created from particles of carbon. Carbon black, for example, is used to give black colour to printing inks. Iron-oxide earth pigments yield ochres (yellow-browns), siennas (orange-browns), and umbers (browns). Certain compounds of chromium are used to provide chrome yellows, oranges, and greens, while various compounds of cadmium yield brilliant yellows, oranges, and reds. Iron, or Prussian, blue and ultramarine blue are the most widely used blue pigments and are both inorganic in origin.

For the most part, organic pigments are presently synthesized from aromatic hydro-carbons. These are compounds containing structures of carbon atoms with hydrogen atoms attached that are formed in closed rings. Organic pigments include azo pigments, which contain a nitrogen group; they account for most of the organic red, orange, and yellow pigments. Copper phthalocyanines provide brilliant, strong blues and greens that are unusually colourfast for organic colours. Some pigments, such as fluorescent ones, are simply dyes that have been rendered insoluble by chemical reaction.

TEMPERA

A tempera medium is dry pigment tempered with an emulsion and thinned with water. The ancient medium was in constant use in most world cultures, until in Europe it was gradually superseded by oil paints during the Renaissance. Tempera was the mural medium in the ancient dynasties of Egypt, Babylonia, Mycenean Greece, and China and was used to decorate the early Christian catacombs. It was employed on a variety of supports, from the stone stelae (or commemorative pillars), mummy cases, and papyrus rolls of ancient Egypt to the wood panels of Byzantine icons and altarpieces and the vellum leaves of medieval illuminated manuscripts.

The word *tempera* originally came from the verb *temper*, "to bring to a desired consistency." Dry pigments are made usable by "tempering" them with a binding and adhesive vehicle. Such painting was distinguished from fresco painting, the colours for which contained no binder. Eventually, after the rise of oil painting, the word gained its present meaning.

True tempera is made by mixture with the yolk of fresh eggs, although manuscript illuminators often used egg white and some easel painters added the whole egg. Other emulsions—such as casein glue with linseed oil, egg yolk with gum and linseed oil, and egg white with linseed or poppy oil—have also been used. Individual painters have experimented with other recipes, but few of those have proved successful; all but William Blake's later tempera paintings on copper sheets, for instance, have darkened and decayed, and it is thought that he mixed his pigment with carpenter's glue.

Distemper is a crude form of tempera made by mixing dry pigment into a paste with water, which is thinned with heated glue in working or by adding pigment to whiting (a mixture of fine-ground chalk and size). It is used for stage scenery and full-size preparatory cartoons for murals and tapestries. When dry, its colours have the pale, matte, powdery quality of pastels, with a similar tendency to smudge. Indeed, damaged cartoons have been retouched with pastel chalks.

Egg tempera is the most-durable form of the medium, being generally unaffected by humidity and temperature. It dries quickly to form a tough film that acts as a protective skin to the support. In handling, in its diversity of transparent and opaque effects, and in the satin sheen of its finish, it resembles the modern acrylic resin emulsion paints.

Traditional tempera painting is a lengthy process. Its supports are smooth surfaces, such as planed wood, fine set plaster, stone, paper, vellum, canvas, and modern composition boards of compressed wood or paper. Linen is generally glued to the surface of panel supports, additional strips masking the seams between braced wood planks. Gesso, a mixture of plaster of paris (or gypsum) with size, is the traditional ground. The first layer is of *gesso grosso*, a mixture of coarse unslaked (not moistened) plaster and size. That provides a rough absorbent surface for 10 or more thin coats of *gesso sottile*, a smooth mixture of size and fine plaster previously slaked in water to retard drying. This laborious preparation results in an opaque, brilliant white, light-reflecting surface similar in texture to hard flat icing sugar.

The design for a large tempera painting was traditionally executed in distemper on a thick paper cartoon. The outlines were pricked with a perforating wheel so that when the cartoon was laid on the surface of the support, the linear pattern was transferred by dabbing, or "pouncing," the perforations with a muslin bag of powdered charcoal. The dotted contours traced through were then fixed in paint. Medieval tempera painters of panels and manuscripts made lavish use of gold leaf on backgrounds and for symbolic features, such as haloes and beams of heavenly light. Areas of the pounced design intended for gilding were first built up into low relief with *gesso duro*, the harder, less-absorbent gesso compound also used for elaborate frame moldings. Background fields were often textured by impressing the *gesso duro*, before it set, with small, carved, intaglio wood blocks to create raised, pimpled, and quilted

Simone Martini used egg tempera on a wooden panel with gold leaf for *Christ Discovered in the Temple* (1342).

repeat patterns that glittered when gilded. Leaves of finely beaten gold were pressed onto a tacky mordant (adhesive compound) or over wet bole (reddish brown earth pigment) that gave greater warmth and depth when the gilded areas were burnished.

Colours were applied with sable brushes in successive broad sweeps or washes of semitransparent tempera. Those dried quickly, preventing the subtle tonal gradations possible with watercolour washes or oil paint; effects of shaded modeling therefore had to be obtained by a crosshatching technique of fine brush strokes. According to the Italian painter Cennino Cennini, the early Renaissance tempera painters laid the colour washes across a fully modeled monochrome underpainting in terre vert (olive-green pigment), a method later developed into the mixed mediums technique of tempera underpainting followed by transparent oil glazes.

The luminous gesso base of a tempera painting, combined with the cumulative effect of overlaid colour washes, produces a unique depth and intensity of colour. Tempera paints dry lighter in value, but their original tonality can be restored by subsequent waxing or varnishing. Other characteristic qualities of a tempera painting, resulting from its fast-drying property and disciplined technique, are its steely lines and crisp edges, its meticulous detail and rich linear textures, and its overall emphasis upon a decorative flat pattern of bold colour masses.

Modern tempera paintings are sometimes varnished or overpainted with thin, transparent oil glazes to produce full, deep-toned results, or they are left unglazed for blond, or light, effects.

Sandro Botticelli's *Primavera* (1477–82), also known as the *Allegory of Spring*, is tempera on wood and is now at the Uffizi Gallery, Florence.

The great tradition of tempera painting was developed in Italy in the 13th and 14th centuries by Duccio di Buoninsegna and Giotto and continued in the work of Giovanni Bellini, Piero della Francesca, Carlo Crivelli, Sandro Botticelli, and Vittore Carpaccio. The 20th century saw a revival of tempera by American artists Ben Shahn, Andrew Wyeth, and Jacob Lawrence and by the British painters Edward Wadsworth and Lucian Freud. Mid-to-late 20th-century artists such as Andy Warhol, Mark Rothko, and David Hockney might have used tempera had it not been replaced mid-century by acrylic paints, which proved more easily and quickly handled.

GESSO

Gesso is a fluid white coating, composed of plaster of paris, chalk, gypsum, or other whiting mixed with glue. It is applied to smooth surfaces such as wood panels, plaster, stone, or canvas to provide the ground for tempera and oil painting or for gilding and painting carved furniture and picture frames. In medieval and Renaissance tempera painting, the surface was covered first with a layer of *gesso grosso* (rough gesso) made with coarse unslaked plaster, then with a series of layers of *gesso sottile* (finishing gesso) made with fine plaster slaked in water, which produced an opaque, white, reflective surface.

In the 14th century, Giotto, the notable Italian painter, used a finishing gesso of parchment glue and slaked plaster of paris. In medieval tempera painting, background areas intended for gilding were built up into low relief with *gesso duro* (hard gesso), a less absorbent composition also used for frame moldings, with patterns often pressed into the gesso with small carved woodblocks. Modern gesso is made of chalk mixed with glue obtained from the skins of rabbits or calves.

FRESCO

Fresco (Italian: "fresh") is the traditional medium for painting directly onto a wall or ceiling. It is the oldest known painting medium, surviving in the prehistoric cave mural decorations and perfected in 16th-century Italy in the *buon'* fresco method.

The cave paintings are thought to date from about 20,000–15,000 BCE. Their pigments probably have been preserved by a natural sinter process of rainwater seeping through the limestone rocks to produce saturated bicarbonate. The colours were rubbed across rock walls and ceilings with sharpened solid lumps of the natural earths (yellow, red, and brown ochre). Outlines were drawn with black sticks of wood charcoal. The discovery of mixing dishes suggests that liquid pigment mixed with fat was also used and smeared with the hand. The subtle tonal gradations of colour on animals painted in the Altamira and Lascaux caves appear to have been dabbed in two stages with fur pads, natural variations on the rock surface being exploited to assist in creating effects of volume. Feathers and frayed twigs may have been used in painting manes and tails.

These were not composite designs but separate scenes and individual studies that, like graffiti drawings, were added at different times, often one on top of another, by various artists. Paintings from approximately 18,000 to 11,000 years ago, during the Magdalenian period, exhibit astonishing powers of accurate observation and ability to represent movement. Women, warriors, horses, bison, bulls, boars, and ibex are depicted in scenes of ritual ceremony, battle, and hunting. Among the earliest images are imprinted and stenciled hands. Vigorous meanders, or "macaroni" linear designs, were traced with fingers dipped in liquid pigment.

FRESCO SECCO

In the *fresco secco* ("dry"), or lime-painting, method, the plastered surface of a wall is soaked with slaked lime. Lime-resistant pigments are applied swiftly before the plaster sets. Secco colours dry lighter than their tone at the time of application, producing the pale, matte, chalky quality of a distempered wall. Although the pigments are fused with the surface, they are not completely absorbed and may flake in time, as in sections of

A detail from Giotto's fresco *Saint Francis before the Sultan (Trial by Fire)* (1297–1300), in the upper church of San Francesco in Assisi, exhibits pigment flaking that sometimes affects works done in *fresco secco.*

Giotto's 14th-century San Francesco murals at Assisi. Secco painting was the prevailing medieval and early Renaissance medium and was revived in 18th-century Europe by artists such as Giovanni Battista Tiepolo, François Boucher, and Jean-Honoré Fragonard.

BUON' FRESCO

Buon', or "true," *fresco* is the most-durable method of painting murals, since the pigments are completely fused with a damp plaster ground to become an integral part of the wall surface. The stone or brick wall is first prepared with a brown *trullisatio* scratch coat, or rough-cast plaster layer. This is then covered by the *arricciato* coat, on which the linear design of the preparatory cartoon (a full-scale drawing) is pounced or engraved by impressing the outlines into the moist, soft plaster with a bone or metal stylus. These lines were usually overworked in reddish sinopia pigment. A thin layer of fine plaster is then evenly spread, allowing the linear design to show through. Before this final *intonaco* ground sets, pigments thinned with water or slaked lime are applied rapidly with calf-hair and hog-bristle brushes; depth of colour is achieved by a succession of quick-drying glazes. Being prepared with slaked lime, the plaster becomes saturated with an aqueous solution of hydrate of lime, which takes up carbonic acid from the air as it soaks into the paint. Carbonate of lime is produced and acts as a permanent pigment binder. Pigment particles crystallize in the plaster, fusing it with the surface to produce the characteristic lustre of *buon'* fresco colours. When dry, these are matte and lighter in tone. Colours are restricted to the range of lime-resistant earth pigments. Mineral colours such as blue, affected by lime, are applied over earth pigment when the plaster is dry.

The *intonaco* coat is laid only across an area sufficient for painting before the plaster sets. The joins between each successive "day piece" are sometimes visible. Alterations must be made by immediate washing or scraping; minor retouching to set plaster is possible with casein or egg tempera, but major corrections necessitate breaking away the *intonaco* and replastering. The swift execution demanded stimulates bold designs in broad masses of colour with a calligraphic vitality of brush marks.

No ancient Greek *buon'* frescoes now exist, but forms of the technique survive in the Pompeian villas of the 1st century CE and earlier, in Chinese tombs at Liaoyang, Manchuria, and in the 6th-century Indian caves at Ajanta. Among the finest *buon'* fresco murals are those by Michelangelo in the Sistine Chapel and by Raphael in the Stanze of the Vatican. Other notable examples from the

Michelangelo used the *buon'* fresco method for the Sistine Chapel frescoes. Paintings are made on wet plaster with the pigments suspended in water so the plaster soaks up the colours and the painting becomes part of the wall.

DIEGO RIVERA

The Mexican painter Diego Rivera (1886–1957) stimulated a revival of fresco painting in Latin America with his bold, large-scale murals.

A government scholarship enabled Rivera to study art at the Academy of San Carlos in Mexico City from age 10, and a grant from the governor of Veracruz enabled him to continue his studies in Europe in 1907. He studied in Spain and in 1909 settled in Paris, where he became a friend of Pablo Picasso, Georges Braque, and other leading modern painters. About 1917 he abandoned the Cubist style in his own work and moved closer to the Post-Impressionism of Paul Cézanne, adopting a visual language of simplified forms and bold areas of colour.

Rivera returned to Mexico in 1921 after meeting with fellow Mexican painter David Alfaro Siqueiros. Both sought to create a new national art on revolutionary themes that would decorate public buildings in the wake of the Mexican Revolution. On returning to Mexico, Rivera painted his first important mural, *Creation*, for the Bolívar Auditorium of the National Preparatory School in Mexico City. In 1923 he began painting the walls of the Ministry of Public Education building in

Mexico City, working in fresco and completing the commission in 1930. These huge frescoes, depicting Mexican agriculture, industry, and culture, reflect a genuinely native subject matter and mark the emergence of Rivera's mature style. Rivera defines his solid, somewhat stylized human figures by precise outlines rather than by internal modeling. The flattened, simplified figures are set in crowded, shallow spaces and are enlivened with bright, bold colours. The Indians, peasants, conquistadores, and factory workers depicted combine monumentality of form with a mood that is lyrical and at times elegiac.

Rivera's next major work was a fresco cycle in a former chapel at what is now the National School of Agriculture at Chapingo (1926–27). His frescoes there contrast scenes of natural fertility and harmony among the pre-Columbian Indians with scenes of their enslavement and brutalization by the Spanish conquerors. Rivera's murals in the Cortés Palace in Cuernavaca (1930) and the National Palace in Mexico City (1930–35) depict various aspects of Mexican history in a more didactic narrative style.

Rivera was in the United States from 1930 to 1934, where he painted murals for the California School of Fine Arts in San Francisco (1931), the Detroit Institute of Arts (1932), and Rockefeller Center in New York

(*CONTINUED ON THE NEXT PAGE*)

(CONTINUED FROM THE PREVIOUS PAGE)

Diego Rivera works on one of his murals that depicts the American "class struggle" in 1933.

City (1933). His *Man at the Crossroads* fresco in Rockefeller Center offended the sponsors because the figure of Vladimir Lenin was in the picture; the work was destroyed by the centre but was later reproduced by Rivera at the Palace of Fine Arts, Mexico City. After returning to Mexico, Rivera continued to paint murals of gradually declining quality. His most ambitious and gigantic mural, an epic on the history of Mexico for the National Palace, Mexico City, was unfinished when he died.

Italian Renaissance can be seen in Florence: painted by Andrea Orcagna in the Museo dell'Opera di Santa Croce, by Gozzoli in the chapel of the Palazzo Medici-Riccardi, and by Domenico Ghirlandaio in the church of Santa Maria Novella. *Buon'* fresco painting is unsuited to the damp, cold climate of northern countries, and there is now some concern for the preservation of frescoes in the sulfurous atmosphere of even many southern cities. *Buon'* fresco was successfully revived by the Mexican mural painters Diego Rivera, José Orozco, and Rufino Tamayo.

SGRAFFITO

Sgraffito (Italian *graffiare*, "to scratch") is a form of fresco painting for exterior walls. A rough plaster undercoat is followed by thin plaster layers, each stained with a different lime-fast colour. These coats are covered by a fine-grain mortar finishing surface. The plaster is then engraved with knives and gouges at different levels to reveal the various coloured layers beneath. The sintered-lime process binds the colours. The surface of modern sgraffito frescoes is often enriched with textures made by impressing nails and machine parts, combined with mosaics of stone, glass, plastic, and metal tesserae.

Sgraffito has been a traditional folk art in Europe since the Middle Ages and was practiced as a fine art in 13th-century Germany. It was revived in updated and modified ways by 20th-century artists such as Max Ernst and Jean Dubuffet.

OIL

Oil paints are made by mixing dry pigment powder with refined linseed oil to a paste, which is then milled

tempera-painting techniques. Basic improvements in the refining of linseed oil and the availability of volatile solvents after 1400 coincided with a need for some other medium than pure egg-yolk tempera to meet the changing requirements of the Renaissance. At first, oil paints and varnishes were used to glaze tempera panels, painted with their traditional linear draftsmanship. The technically brilliant, jewel-like portraits of the 15th-century Flemish painter Jan van Eyck, for example, were done in this way.

In the 16th century, oil colour emerged as the basic painting material in Venice. By the end of the century, Venetian artists had become proficient in the exploitation of the basic characteristics of oil painting, particularly in their use of successive layers of glazes. Linen canvas, after a long period of development, replaced wooden panels as the most popular support.

The tempera-underpainting-oil-glaze technique was practiced into the 17th century. Artists such as Italian painter Titian, Spanish painter El Greco, Flemish painter Peter Paul Rubens, and Spanish painter Diego Velázquez, however, used oil pigments alone and, employing a method similar to pastel painting, applied them directly to the brownish ground with which they had tinted the white priming. Velázquez's highly economical but informative brushstrokes have frequently been emulated, especially in portraiture. Rubens influenced later painters in the manner in which he loaded his light colours, opaquely, in juxtaposition to thin, transparent darks and shadows. Another master of oil painting was the Dutch painter Rembrandt van Rijn. In his work a single brushstroke can effectively depict form; cumulative strokes give great textural depth, combining the rough and the smooth, the thick and the thin. A system of loaded whites and

In Rembrandt's *Portrait of the Artist at His Easel* (1660) broad applications of paint and brushstrokes can be seen, especially in the white cap. Sometimes Rembrandt used a palette knife to apply paint.

transparent darks is further enhanced by glazed effects, blendings, and highly controlled impastos.

These 17th-century masters' works had contours and shadows that were stained in streaks and washes of diluted paint, while lighter areas were created with dry, opaque scumbles, the tinted ground meanwhile providing the halftones and often remaining untouched for passages of local or reflected colour in the completed picture. This use of oil paint was particularly suited to expressing atmospheric effects and to creating chiaroscuro, or light and dark, patterns. It also encouraged a bravura handling of paint, where stabs, flourishes, lifts, and pressures of the brush economically described the most subtle changes of form, texture, and colour according to the influence exerted by the tinted ground through the varying thicknesses of overlaid pigment. This method was still practiced by the 19th-century painters, such as John Constable, J.M.W. Turner, Eugène Delacroix, and Honoré Daumier. The Impressionists, however, found the luminosity of a brilliant white ground essential to the alla prima technique with which they represented the colour intensities and shifting lights of their plein-air (open-air) subjects. Most oil paintings since then have been executed on white surfaces.

The rapid deterioration of Leonardo's 15th-century *Last Supper* (last restored 1978–99), which was painted in oils on plaster, may have deterred later artists from using the medium directly on a wall surface. The likelihood of eventual warping also prohibited using the large number of braced wood panels required to make an alternative support for an extensive mural painting in oils. Because canvas can be woven to any length and because an oil-painted surface is elastic, mural paintings could be executed in the studio and rolled and restretched on a wooden framework at the site or marouflaged (fastened with an adhesive) directly onto a wall surface. In addition to the immense studio canvases painted for particular sites by artists such as Jacopo Tintoretto, Paolo Veronese, Delacroix, Pierre-Cécile Puvis de Chavannes, and Claude Monet, the use of canvas has made it possible for mural-size, modern oil paintings to be transported for exhibition to all parts of the world.

The tractable nature of the oil medium has sometimes encouraged slipshod craftsmanship. Working over partly dry pigment or priming may produce a wrinkled surface. The excessive use of oil as a vehicle causes colours to yellow and darken, while cracking, blooming, powdering, and flaking can result from poor priming, overthinning with turpentine, or the use of varnish dryers and other spirits. Colour changes may also occur through the use of chemically incompatible pigment mixtures or from the fading of fugitive synthetic hues, such as crimson lakes, the brilliant red pigment favoured by Pierre-Auguste Renoir.

The technical requirements of some schools of modern painting cannot be realized by traditional genres and techniques, however, and some abstract painters, and to some extent contemporary painters in traditional styles, have expressed a need for an entirely different plastic flow or viscosity that cannot be had with oil paint and its conventional additives. Some require a greater range of thick and thin applications and a more rapid rate of drying. Some artists have mixed coarsely grained materials with their colours to create new textures, some have used oil paints in much heavier thicknesses than before, and many have turned to the use of acrylic paints, which are more versatile and dry rapidly.

IMPASTO

Impasto is paint that is applied to a canvas or panel in quantities that make it stand out from the surface. Impasto was used frequently to mimic the broken-textured quality of highlights—i.e., the surfaces of objects that are struck by an intense light. Impasto came into its own in the 17th century, when such Baroque painters as Rembrandt, Frans Hals, and Diego Velázquez used skillfully and minutely worked impastos to depict lined and wrinkled skin or the sparkle of elaborately crafted armour, jewelry, and rich fabrics. The 19th-century painter Vincent van Gogh made notable use of impastos, building up and defining the forms in his paintings with thick, nervous dabs of paint. Twentieth-century painters such as Jackson Pollock and Willem de Kooning often applied impastos with a dynamism and a gestural bravura that emphasized the physical qualities of the paint itself. Since then, raw pigments applied thickly to a canvas have become a staple technique of modern abstract and semifigurative painting.

WATERCOLOUR

Watercolours are pigments ground with gum arabic and gall and thinned with water in use. Sable- and squirrel-("camel") hair brushes are used on white or tinted paper and card.

Three hundred years before the late 18th-century English watercolourists, German artist Albrecht Dürer anticipated their technique of transparent colour washes in a remarkable series of plant studies and panoramic landscapes. Until the emergence of the English school, however, watercolour became a medium merely for colour tinting outlined drawings or, combined with opaque body colour to produce effects similar to gouache or tempera, was used in preparatory studies for oil paintings.

The chief exponents of the English method were Thomas Girtin, John Sell Cotman, John Robert Cozens, Richard Parkes Bonington, David Cox, and Constable. Turner, however, true to his unorthodox genius, added white to his watercolour and used rags, sponges, and knives to obtain unique effects of light and texture. Victorian watercolourists, such as Birket Foster, used a laborious method of colour washing a monochrome underpainting, similar in principle to the tempera-oil technique. Following the direct, vigorous watercolours of the French Impressionists and Post-Impressionists, however, the medium was established in Europe and America as an expressive picture medium in its own right. Notable 20th-century water-colourists were Wassily Kandinsky, Paul Klee, Raoul Dufy, and Georges Rouault; the U.S. artists Winslow Homer, Thomas Eakins, Maurice Prendergast, Charles Burchfield, John Marin, Lyonel Feininger, and

In *Lower Manhattan* (1923), a watercolour on paper, John Marin uses Cubist abstraction and fragmentation to impart energy and emotion in this view of New York City.

Jim Dine; and the English painters John and Paul Nash.

In the "pure" watercolour technique, often referred to as the English method, no white or other opaque pigment is applied, colour intensity and tonal depth being built up by successive, transparent washes on damp paper. Patches of white paper are left unpainted to represent white objects and to create effects of reflected light. These flecks of bare paper produce the sparkle characteristic of pure watercolour. Tonal gradations and soft, atmospheric qualities are rendered by staining the paper when it is very wet with varying proportions of pigment. Sharp accents, lines, and coarse textures are introduced when the paper has dried. The paper should be of the type sold as "handmade from rags"; this is generally thick and grained. Cockling is avoided when the surface dries out if the dampened paper has been first stretched across a special frame or held in position during painting by an edging of tape.

Watercolour compares in range and variety with any other painting method. Transparent watercolour allows for a freshness and luminosity in its washes and for a deft calligraphic brushwork that makes it a most alluring medium. There is one basic difference between transparent watercolour and all other heavy painting mediums—its transparency. The oil painter can paint one opaque colour over another until he has achieved his desired result. The whites are created with opaque white. The watercolourist's approach is the opposite. In essence, instead of building up he leaves out. The white paper creates the whites. The darkest accents may be placed on the paper with the pigment as it comes out of the tube or with very little water mixed with it. Otherwise the colours are diluted with water. The more water in

JOHN MARIN

John Marin (1870–1953) was an American painter and printmaker especially known for his expressionistic watercolour seascapes of Maine and his views of Manhattan.

After working as an architectural draftsman, Marin studied painting at the Pennsylvania Academy of the Fine Arts in Philadelphia and at the Art Students League of New York City. In 1905 he went to Europe, where he was influenced by the watercolours and etchings of James McNeill Whistler. Marin remained largely unaware of the new movements in European art until 1910, when he returned to New York. There, at Alfred Stieglitz's "291" gallery and at the Armory Show in 1913, he became familiar with Cubism and the various schools of German Expressionism. Influenced by those movements, his own style matured into a very personal form of expressionism, exemplified in works such as *The Singer Building* (1921) and *Maine Islands* (1922).

Artists usually employ watercolour to produce only delicate, transparent effects, but Marin's brilliant command of the medium enabled him to render the monumental power of New York and the relentless surge of the sea on the Maine coast. His concern with force and motion led him to produce works such as *Lower Manhattan* (1922) and *Off York Island, Maine* (1922), in which objective reality is hardly recognizable amid the activity of the canvas.

From the 1930s Marin increasingly painted with oils. In works using this medium, such as *Tunk Mountains, Maine* (1945), he often employed the watercolour technique of dragging a nearly dry brush across the canvas to achieve an effect of lightness and transparency.

the wash, the more the paper affects the colours; for example, vermilion, a warm red, will gradually turn into a cool pink as it is thinned with more water.

The dry-brush technique—the use of the brush containing pigment but little water, dragged over the rough surface of the paper—creates various granular effects similar to those of crayon drawing. Whole compositions can be made in this way. This technique also may be used over dull washes to enliven them.

INK

Ink is the traditional painting medium of China and Japan, where it has been used with long-haired brushes of wolf, goat, or badger on silk or absorbent paper. Asian black ink is a gum-bound carbon stick that is ground on rough stone and mixed with varying amounts of water to create a wide range of modulated tones or applied almost dry, with lightly brushed strokes, to

SUIBOKU-GA

Suiboku-ga, also called Sumi-e, is Japanese monochrome ink painting, a technique first developed in China during the Sung dynasty (960–1274) and taken to Japan by Zen Buddhist monks in the mid-14th century. Although generally content to copy Chinese models, early Japanese artists also excelled in the field of portraiture and figure painting. Suiboku-ga reached its height in the Muromachi period (1338–1573) with such masters as Sesshū Tōyō, whose landscapes were uniquely Japanese, and Sesson Shūkei, who worked in the far northeast of Japan.

The bold use of black ink strokes and washes allowed suiboku-ga artists to eliminate from their paintings all but the essential character of their subject, an aim closely related to the pursuit of Zen Buddhism. Although suiboku-ga was popular well into the Tokugawa period (1603–1867), it soon lost its spontaneity and became formalistic in style.

produce coarser textures. The calligraphic brush technique is expressive of Zen Buddhist and Confucian philosophies, brush-stroke formulas for the spiritual interpretation of nature in painting dictating the use of the lifted brush tip for the "bone," or "lean," structure of things and the spreading belly of the hairs for their "flesh," or "fat," volumes. The East Asian artist poises the brush vertically above the paper and controls its rhythmic movements from the shoulder. Distant forms represented in landscapes painted on silk were sometimes brushed on from the reverse side.

In the Western world, ink has been used rather more for preparatory studies and topographical and literary illustrations than as a medium for easel paintings. Western artists have generally combined ink washes with contours and textures in quill or steel pen. Among the finest of these are by Rembrandt, Nicolas Poussin, Francisco Goya, Samuel Palmer, Constable, and Édouard Manet. Claude Lorrain, Turner, and Daumier and, in the 20th century, Braque, Picasso, Reginald Marsh, Henri Michaux, and John Piper are some of those who have exploited its unique qualities. Modern artists also use ballpoint and felt pens.

GOUACHE

Gouache is opaque watercolour, known also as poster paint and designer's colour. It is thinned with water for applying, with sable- and hog-hair brushes, to white or tinted paper and card and, occasionally, to silk. Honey, starch, or acrylic is sometimes added to retard its quick-drying property. Liquid glue is preferred as a thinner by painters wishing to retain the tonality of colours (which otherwise dry slightly lighter in key) and to prevent thick paint from flaking. Gouache paints have the advantages that they dry out almost immediately to a matte finish and, if required, without visible brush marks. These qualities, with the capacities to be washed thinly or applied in thick impasto and a wide colour range that now includes fluorescent and metallic pigments, make the medium particularly suited to preparatory studies for oil and acrylic paintings. It is the medium that produces the suede finish and crisp lines characteristic of many Indian and Islamic miniatures, and it has been used in Western screen and fan decoration and by modern artists such as Rouault, Klee, Jean Dubuffet, and Morris Graves.

ENCAUSTIC

Encaustic painting (from the Greek: "burnt in") was the ancient method, recorded by 1st-century Roman scholar Pliny the Elder, of fixing pigments with heated wax. It was probably first practiced in Egypt about 3000 BCE and is thought to have reached its peak in Classical Greece, although no examples from that period survive. Pigments, mixed with melted beeswax, were brushed onto stone or plaster, smoothed with a metal spatula, and then blended and driven into the wall with a heated iron. The surface was later polished with a cloth. Leonardo and others attempted unsuccessfully to revive the technique. North American Indians used an encaustic method whereby pigments mixed with hot animal fat were pressed into a design engraved on smoothed buffalo hide.

A simplified encaustic technique uses a spatula to apply wax mixed with solvent and pigment to wood or canvas, producing a ridged, impasto surface. This is an ancient and most durable medium. Coptic mummy portraits from the 1st and 2nd centuries CE retain the softly blended, translucent colouring typical of wax-work effigies. In the 19th century Vincent van Gogh also used this method to give body to his oil pigment; the Neo-Impressionist artist Louis Hayet applied encaustic to paper, and it was used by U.S. painter Jasper Johns for his iconic paintings of maps, targets, and flags. Coloured wax crayons have also been used by modern painters such as Picasso, Klee, Arshile Gorky, and Hockney.

CASEIN

Casein, or "cheese painting," is a medium in which pigments are tempered with the gluey curd of cheese or milk precipitate. For handling, an emulsion of casein and lime is thinned with water. The active element of casein contains nitrogen, which forms a soluble caseate of calcium in the presence of lime. It is applied in thin washes to rigid surfaces, such as cardboard, wood, and plastered walls.

Refined, pure, powdered casein, which can be dissolved with ammonia, has been used for easel and mural paintings since the latter 19th and early 20th centuries, and, more recently, ready-made casein paints in tubes have come into very wide use. An advantage of casein painting is that it can create effects that approach those of oil painting. It permits the use of bristle brushes and a moderate impasto, like oil painting, but not the fusion of tones. It is preferred by some because of speedy drying and matte effects. When dry, the paint becomes water resistant to a considerable degree. Casein paintings may be varnished to further resemble oil paintings, and they are frequently glazed or overpainted with oil colours. Because casein is too brittle for canvas, it must be applied to rigid boards or panels.

Casein paints were used in ancient Rome. They are now available ready-made in tubes and have been used by such modern artists as Robert Motherwell and Claes Oldenburg.

Casein is also an ingredient of some charcoal and pastel fixatives and was a traditional primer for walls and panels.

SYNTHETIC AND OTHER MEDIUMS

Synthetic mediums, developed by industrial research, range from the Liquitex fabric dyes used on canvas by U.S. abstract painter Larry Poons to the house enamel paints employed at times by Picasso and Jackson Pollock.

The most popular medium and the first to challenge the supremacy of oils is acrylic resin emulsion, since this plastic paint combines most of the expressive capabilities of oils with the quick-drying properties of tempera and gouache. It is made by mixing pigments with a synthetic resin and thinning with water. It can be applied to any sufficiently toothed surface with brush, roller, airbrush, spatula, sponge, or rag. Acrylic paints dry quickly, without brush marks, to form a matte, waterproof film that is also elastic, durable, and easily cleaned. They show little colour change in drying, nor do they darken in time. While they lack the surface textural richness of oil or encaustic, they can be built up with a spatula into opaque impastos or thinned immediately into transparent colour glazes. Polyvinyl acetate (PVA) or synthetic gesso is applied for priming, although it is claimed that acrylic paints can be safely applied directly onto unprepared raw canvas or cotton. The wide range of intense hues is extended by fluorescent and metallic pigments. Acrylic paints became immediately popular with artists when they were first commercially promoted in the 1960s. Notable 20th-century artists who used acrylic paint include Pop artists Andy Warhol and Roy Lichtenstein. Polymer paints are particularly suitable for the precise, immaculate finish demanded by Op art, Minimalist, and Photo-realist painters such as Bridget Riley, Morris Louis, Frank Stella, and Richard Estes, and colour-field artists such as Mark Rothko, Ellsworth Kelly, Barnett Newman, and David Hockney.

FRENCH PASTELS

Among other mediums are French pastels. French pastels, with the sharpened lumps of pigment used by Ice Age artists, are the purest and most direct painting materials. Pastel pigments are mixed only with sufficient gum to bind them for drying into stick molds. Generally, they are used on raw strawboard or on coarse-grained tinted paper, although vellum, wood, and canvas have been also employed. These colours will not fade or darken, but, since they are not absorbed by the surface of the support, they lie as pigment powder and are easily smudged. Unfortunately, pastel colours lose their luminosity and tonality if fixed with a varnish and so are best preserved in deep mounts behind glass. Edgar Degas often overcame the fragile nature of true pastel painting by the unorthodox method of working on turpentine-soaked paper, which absorbed the powdery pigment.

Eighteenth-century portrait pastellists, such as Maurice-Quentin de La Tour, Jean-Baptiste Peronneau, Jean-Étienne Liotard, Rosalba Carriera, and Anton Raphael Mengs, blended the pigment with coiled paper stumps so the surface resembled that of a smooth oil painting. Later pastel painters, such as Degas, Henri de Toulouse-Lautrec, Mary Cassatt, Everett Shinn, Odilon Redon, and Arthur Dove, contrasted broad masses of granular colour, spread with the side of the stick, with broken contours and passages of loose cross-hatching and smudging. They often used the tinted ground as a halftone, and, according to the amount of manual pressure exerted on the chalk, they varied the degree of pigment opacity to extract a wide range of tints and shades from each pastel colour.

Edgar Degas's *Dancers* (c. 1905) is an oil pastel drawing. Degas created many of his ballet dancer works with French pastels and oils.

ARTHUR G. DOVE

Arthur G. Dove (1880–1946) was an American painter who was one of the earliest nonobjective artists.

Dove graduated from Cornell University in 1903. He began his career as a magazine illustrator, and his early work appeared in *Scribner's*, *Collier's*, and *The Saturday Evening Post*. In 1907–08 he traveled to Paris to study. While there, he befriended many other American artists, including Max Weber and Alfred Maurer, and was influenced by Impressionism, Fauvism, and the work of Paul Cézanne. He exhibited twice in the Salon d'Automne. In 1909 he returned to the United States, met photographer Alfred Stieglitz, and–together with John Marin and Georgia O'Keeffe–became an artist whom Stieglitz championed at 291, his gallery in New York City. Dove exhibited there in 1910, by which time he had fully embraced abstract art.

Dove's art reflects his belief that colour and form are instruments with which to express the essence beneath the physical exterior of things; his shapes are typically amorphous, his colours muted. *In Foghorns* (1929), for example, he used size-graduated shapes and gradations of hue to express visually the sound of foghorns. Despite their nonobjective character, his paintings often suggest the undulating qualities of landscape and the forms of nature. Dove also created many ironic collages, such as *Goin' Fishin'* (1925), made of a variety of materials. He worked extensively in pastels throughout the 1920s and experimented with a variety of graphic media.

OIL PASTELS

Oil pastels are pigments ground in mastic with a variety of oils and waxes. They are used in a similar way to that of French pastels but are already fixed and harder, producing a permanent, waxy finish. Oil-pastel paintings are generally executed on white paper, card, or canvas. The colours can be blended if the surface of the support is dampened with turpentine or if they are overworked with turpentine. They are popular for small preparatory studies for paintings.

GLASS PAINTINGS

Glass paintings are executed with oil and hard resin or with watercolour and gum on glass sheets. These have been a folk art tradition in Europe and North America and, from the 15th to the 18th century, were regarded as a fine art in northern Europe, where they have been more recently revived by such painters as Willi Dirx, Ida Kerkovius, Lily Hildebrandt, Klee, Oskar Schlemmer, and Heinrich Campendonck. Colours are applied from the back in reverse order. Unpainted areas of glass are often coated with mercury, providing a mirror background to the coloured images. That treatment creates the kind of illusionary, bizarre spatial relationship between the viewer and picture space sought by Italian artist Michelangelo Pistoletto with his use of photographic images fixed to a polished steel sheet. The colours seen through glass appear translucent, jewel-like, and, since they cannot be touched, even magical.

IVORY PAINTING

Ivory painting was practiced in the 18th and 19th centuries in Europe and America for portrait miniatures. These were generally oval-shaped and designed as keepsakes, lockets, and mantle pictures. They were painted under a magnifying glass in fairly dry watercolour or tempera stippling, with sable- or marten-hair brushes on thin, semitranslucent ivory pieces. Corrections were made with a needle. The velvet quality of their colours was enhanced, on the thinner ivories, by the glow produced by a gold leaf or tinted backing.

LACQUER

Lacquer has been a traditional Chinese medium for more than 2,000 years. It combines painting with intaglio relief. Linen-covered wood panels are coated with chalk or clay, followed by many thin layers of black or red lacquer tree resin. The surface is polished and a design engraved, which is then coloured and gilded or inset with mother-of-pearl. Layers of compressed paper or molded papier-mâché have also provided supports. In China and Japan, lacquer has been used principally for decorating shrine panels, screens, caskets, panniers (large baskets), and musical instruments.

SAND, OR DRY, PAINTING

Sand, or dry, painting is a traditional religious art of the North American Indians, and exists in highly developed forms among the Navajos and Pueblo Indians of the American Southwest and in simpler forms among several Plains and California Indian tribes. It is still practiced in healing ceremonies among the Navajos of New Mexico and Arizona. Ground sandstone, natural ochres, mineral earths, and powdered charcoal are sprinkled onto a pattern marked into an area covered with yellow-white sand. About 600 different pictures are known, consisting of various representations of deities, animals, lightning, rainbows, plants, and other symbols described in the chants that accompany various rites. In healing, the choice of the particular painting is left to the curer. Upon completion of the picture, the patient sits on the centre of the painting, and sand from the painting is applied to parts of his body. When the ritual is completed, the painting is destroyed. These "floor" pictures influenced Jackson Pollock in his horizontally spread action paintings.

For years the Indians would not allow permanent, exact copies of sand paintings to be made. When the designs were copied in rugs, an error was deliberately made so that the original design would still be powerful. Today many of the paintings have been copied both to preserve the art and for the record.

PAPER

From the end of the 18th century, profiles and full-length group portraits were cut in black paper, mounted on white card, and often highlighted in gold or white. A silhouette ("shade") might be first outlined from the sitter's cast shadow with the aid of a physionotrace. American artist Kara Walker revived the silhouette technique with a series of controversial works that commented on race, gender, and class.

KARA WALKER

American installation artist Kara Walker (b. 1969) uses intricate cut-paper silhouettes, together with collage, drawing, painting, performance, film, video, shadow puppetry, light projection, and animation, to comment on power, race, and gender relations.

Her father, Larry Walker, was an artist and chair of the art department at the University of the Pacific in Stockton. She showed promise as an artist from a young age, but it was not until the family moved to Georgia when she was 13 that she began to focus on issues of race. Walker received a bachelor's degree (1991) from the Atlanta College of Art and a master's degree (1994) from the Rhode Island School of Design, where she began working in the silhouette form while exploring themes of slavery, violence, and sex found in sources such as books, films, and cartoons.

In 1994 Walker's work appeared in a new-talent show at the Drawing Center in New York. Her contribution was a 50-foot (15-metre) mural of life-size silhouettes depicting a set of disturbing scenes set in the antebellum American South. The piece was titled *Gone, an Historical Romance of a Civil War as It Occurred Between the Dusky Thighs of One Negress and Her Heart*. That work and subsequent others, such as a series of watercolours titled *Negress Notes* (*Brown Follies*) (1996–97), caused a stir. Some African American artists, particularly those who participated in the civil rights movement, deplored her use of racist caricatures. Walker made it clear that her intent as an artist was not to create pleasing images or to raise questions with easy answers. She also explained her use of the silhouette by stating that "the silhouette says a lot with very little information, but that's also what the stereotype does."

(CONTINUED ON THE NEXT PAGE)

(CONTINUED FROM THE PREVIOUS PAGE)

In 1997, at age 27, Walker received a John D. and Catherine T. MacArthur Foundation "genius grant." Her work was exhibited in galleries and museums worldwide, and she served as the U.S. representative to the 2002 São Paulo Biennial. She was also on the faculty of the School of the Arts at Columbia University in New York City.

In 2006 the Metropolitan Museum of Art in New York City featured her exhibition titled "After the Deluge," which was inspired in part by the devastation wreaked the previous year by Hurricane Katrina in New Orleans.

Kara Walker stands before *Gone, An Historical Romance of a Civil War as It Occurred Between the Dusky Thighs of One Young Negress and Her Heart* (1994) at the Museum of Modern Art in New York City in 2010.

The exhibition juxtaposed pieces from the museum's own collection—many of which depicted black figures or images demonstrating the terrific power of water—with some of her own works. The intermingled disparate images created an amalgam of new meaning fraught with a discomfiting ambiguity characteristic of much of Walker's output. Two subsequent major exhibitions were "My Complement, My Enemy, My Oppressor, My Love," a comprehensive traveling show organized in 2007 by the Walker Art Center in Minneapolis, Minnesota, and "Rise Up Ye Mighty Race!" (2013), for the Art Institute of Chicago. In 2015 Walker had her first London show entitled "Go to Hell or Atlanta, Whichever Comes First" at Victoria Miro Gallery, in which her works continue to explore the violent histories of colonialism and slavery.

COLLAGE

Collage was the Dada and Synthetic Cubist technique of combining labels, tickets, newspaper cuttings, wallpaper scraps, and other "found" surfaces with painted textures. Among the most lyrical and inventive works in this magpie medium are the so-called Merz collages by Kurt Schwitters. Frottage was Max Ernst's method of taking paper rubbings from surfaces, unrelated to one another in real life, and combining them to create fantasy landscapes. Cut paper shapes, hand coloured in gouache, were used by Matisse for his monumental last paintings; Piet Mondrian composed his famous *Victory Boogie Woogie* (1942–43) in coloured-paper cutouts.

MECHANICAL MEDIUMS

The use of mechanical mediums in painting has run parallel to similar developments in modern music and drama. In the field of cybernetics, painters have programmed computers to permutate drawings, photographs, diagrams, and symbols through sequences of progressive distortion; and light patterns are produced on television screens by deliberate magnetic interference and by sound-wave oscillations. Artists have also explored the expressive and aesthetic possibilities of linear holograms, in which all sides of an object can be shown by superimposed light images. Painters are among those who have extended the boundaries of filmmaking as an art form. Examples include the Surrealist film fantasies created by Berthold Bartosch, Jean Cocteau, Hans Richter, and Salvador Dalí, by Oskar Schlemmer's filmed ballets and Norman McLaren's hand-painted abstract animations.

For some Conceptual artists, language was the medium. Words themselves—spelled out in neon or LED lights or projected on gallery or public walls—served as art for artists such as Joseph Kosuth, Lawrence Weiner, and Jenny Holzer.

MIXED MEDIUMS

Some pictures are first painted in one medium and cor-
rected or enriched with colour and texture in another.
Examples of this kind of mixed mediums are the
Renaissance tempera-oil technique, William Blake's
relief etchings colour-printed in glue tempera and
hand-finished in watercolour, and Degas's overpainted
monotypes and his combinations of pastel, gouache,
and oil. More recent examples are Richard Hamilton's
photographs overpainted in oil colour, Dubuffet's patch-
work assemblages of painted canvas and paper, and
Klee's alchemy in mixing ingredients such as oil and
distemper on chalk over jute and watercolour and wax
on muslin stuck on wood.

FORMS OF PAINTING

There are many forms of painting, both in Eastern and Western art, including mural painting, easel and panel painting, miniature painting, manuscript illumination, scroll painting, screen and fan painting, panoramas, and some modern forms.

MURAL PAINTING

Mural painting has its roots in the primeval instincts of people to decorate their surroundings and to use wall surfaces as a form for expressing ideas, emotions, and beliefs. In their universal manifestation in graffiti and in ancient murals, such as cave paintings and protodynastic Egyptian frescoes, symbols and representational images have been spread freely and indiscriminately across walls, ceilings, and floors. But, in more disciplined attempts to symbolize the importance and function of particular buildings through their interior decoration, murals have been designed for the restricted framework of specific surface areas. They therefore have to be painted in close relationship to the scale, style, and mood of the interior and with regard to such siting considerations as light sources, eye levels, the spectators' lines of sight and means of approach, and the emotive scale relationship between spectators and the painted images.

Early mural decorations for tombs, temples, sanctuaries, and catacombs were generally designed in horizontal divisions and vertical axes. These grid patterns were in harmony with the austere character of the interiors, and their geometrical plan enabled the artist to depict clearly the various episodes and symbols of a narrative subject. In these early traditions of mural design, in China, India, Mexico, Egypt, Crete, and Byzantium, no illusionary devices were used to deny the true flatness of the wall surface; images were silhouetted against a flatly painted ground framed by decorative dadoes (the decoration adorning the lower part of an interior wall) of stylized motifs in repeat patterns. By the early Renaissance, however, innovators such as Giotto, Masaccio, and Fra Angelico were placing figures within architectural and landscape settings, painted as if extensions to the real dimensions of the interior. The

Fra Angelico placed the figures of the Virgin Mary and the angel Gabriel within architectural and landscape settings in the fresco *The Annunciation* (1438–45). By doing so, he extended visually the interior space of the priory of San Marco in Florence.

peak of technical skill and artistic expression was reached in the 15th and 16th centuries with the frescoes of Piero della Francesca, Michelangelo, and Raphael. The irregular shapes of wall areas and the distortions produced by convex surfaces were inventively exploited in the design. Intruding doors and windows, for example, were skillfully circumvented by sweeping pattern rhythms or were incorporated as features in the painting, and figures were foreshortened so as to appear to float across or to rise into cupolas (rounded vaults that form ceilings), lunettes (rounded spaces over doors or windows), and apses (domed projections of a church, usually at the east end or altar), the curving surfaces of which might be painted to simulate celestial skies. Existing structural wall features provided the divisions between narrative episodes. These were often supplemented by trompe l'oeil ("deceive the eye") columns, pilasters, arcading, balustrading, steps, and other architectural forms that also served to fuse the painted setting with the real interior. (European painters from the early Renaissance onward occasionally fostered illusionism by painting false frames out of which the contents of a still life or portrait appeared to spill or by creating windowlike images suggesting actual openings in the wall or ceiling.)

With the increasing dependence upon tapestry hangings and stained glass as primary forms of interior decoration, mural painting suffered a decline in the Western world. Except for those given to Rubens, Tiepolo, Delacroix, and Puvis de Chavannes, there were relatively few important mural commissions in the period following the High Renaissance. In the

This mural in New York City is a recreation of an original painted by Keith Haring in 1982. The original mural lasted only a few months because Haring's Day-Glo colours started to break down in the sunshine.

20th century, however, enlightened patronage occasionally enabled leading modern artists to execute paintings for specific sites: Monet's *Water-Lilies* series for the Paris Orangerie, for example, and other murals in France by Vuillard, Matisse, Léger, Chagall, and Picasso; in Mexico and the United States by Orozco, Rivera, Tamayo, and David Siqueiros, and also in the United States by Matisse, Ben Shahn, Keith Haring, and Willem de Kooning; in Britain by Sir Stanley Spencer and Edward Bawden; in Norway by Edvard Munch; in the Netherlands by Karel Appel; and in Italy by Afro Basaldella.

GRAFFITI AND KEITH HARING

American graphic artist and designer Keith Haring (1958–1990) popularized some of the strategies and impulses of graffiti art. Derived from the Italian word *graffio* ("scratch"), graffiti ("incised inscriptions," plural but often used as singular) has a long history. For example, markings have been found in ancient Roman ruins, in the remains of the Mayan city of Tikal in Central America, on rocks in Spain dating to the 16th century, and in medieval English churches. During the 20th century, graffiti in the United States and Europe was closely associated with gangs, who used it for a variety of purposes: for identifying or claiming territory, for memorializing dead gang members in an informal "obituary," for boasting about acts (e.g., crimes) committed by gang members, and for challenging rival gangs as a prelude to violent confrontations. Graffiti was particularly prominent in major urban centres throughout the world, especially in the United States and Europe; common targets were subways, billboards, and walls. In the 1990s there emerged a new form of graffiti, known as "tagging," which entailed the repeated use of a single symbol or series of symbols to mark territory.

To attract the most attention possible, this type of graffiti usually appeared in strategically or centrally located neighbourhoods.

To some observers graffiti is a form of public art, continuing the tradition, for example, of the murals commissioned by the U.S. Works Progress Administration Federal Art Project during the Great Depression and the work of Diego Rivera in Mexico. Like the murals of these artists, great works of graffiti can beautify a neighbourhood and speak to the interests of a specific community. For example, the graffiti in many Hispanic neighbourhoods in the United States is quite elaborate and is regarded by many as a form of urban art. The question of whether such work is an innovative art form or a public nuisance has aroused much debate.

Graffiti became notoriously prominent in New York City in the late 20th century. Large elaborate multicoloured graffiti created with spray paint on building walls and subway cars came to define the urban landscape. The art world's fascination with artists who functioned outside traditional gallery channels stimulated an interest in this form of self-expression. In the 1980s New York artists such as Keith Haring and Jean-Michel Basquiat gained notoriety for their graffiti and parlayed this recognition into successful careers as painters represented by top galleries.

(CONTINUED ON THE NEXT PAGE)

(CONTINUED FROM THE PREVIOUS PAGE)

After a brief period studying at the Ivy School of Art in Pittsburgh, Haring moved to New York City in 1978 to attend the School of Visual Arts. With fellow artists Kenny Scharf and Jean-Michel Basquiat, Haring immersed himself in the punk clubs and street art scene of New York. In 1981 he began drawing graffiti—unauthorized chalk drawings on blank black advertising panels—in the New York subways. These would eventually number in the thousands, and they quickly created a popular following for his lively figural and patterned imagery and his cheekily outlaw activity. Haring shared few of the "tagging" tactics of urban graffitists, being drawn instead to the possibilities of a new public and vernacular kind of signage.

He began making large outdoor murals, eventually executing them in Rio de Janeiro, Berlin, Melbourne, Chicago, Atlanta, and elsewhere, often assisted by scores of children. Haring's ebullient personality, infectious sense of play, and universally understood hieroglyphic style brought him attention from the mainstream press and transferred easily into his work in music videos and fashion design.

Haring was socially conscious, and his murals often reflected his position on social issues. He sought to raise awareness of AIDS and fought against the proliferation of illegal drugs.

EASEL AND PANEL PAINTING

The easel, or studio, picture was a form developed during the Renaissance with the establishment of the painter as an individual artist. Its scale and portability enabled European artists to extend the range of themes, previously restricted to those suitable to mural decoration. Easel and panel forms include still life, portraiture, landscape, and genre subjects and permit the representation of ephemeral effects of light and atmosphere that the more intimate forms of Asian art had already allowed the painters of scrolls, screens, and fans to express. Although easel paintings are occasionally commissioned for a special purpose, they are generally bought as independent art objects and used as decorative focal features or illusionary window views in private homes. They are also collected as financial investment, for social prestige, for the therapeutic escapism their subject may provide, or purely for the aesthetic pleasure they afford.

Panel paintings, by strict definition, are small pictures designed for specific sacred or secular purposes or as part of a functional object. Although these wooden boards are sometimes categorized as a form of "decorative" rather than "fine" art, the best examples justify their place in museums alongside great easel paintings. Among the functions they originally served were as predellas (the facings to altar-step risers); devotional and ceremonial icons; portable, folding diptych and triptych altarpieces; shop and tavern signboards; mummy cases; and panel decorations of carriages, musical instruments, and cassoni. Many of them were painted by acknowledged masters, such as Fra Angelico, Paolo Uccello, and Antoine Watteau, as well as by anonymous folk artists.

PLEIN-AIR PAINTING

In its strictest sense, plein-air painting is the practice of painting landscape pictures out-of-doors; more loosely, it is the achievement of an intense impression of the open air (French: *plein air*) in a landscape painting.

Until the time of the painters of the Barbizon school in mid-19th-century France, it was normal practice to execute rough sketches of landscape subjects in the open air and produce finished paintings in the studio. Part of this was a matter of convenience. Before the invention of the collapsible tin paint tube, widely marketed by the colour merchants Winsor & Newton in 1841, painters purchased their colours in the form of ground pigment and mixed them fresh with an appropriate medium such as oil. The new tubes filled with prepared colours, as well as the invention of a lightweight, portable easel a decade later, made it much easier to paint out-of-doors. Despite these advances, many of the Barbizon painters continued to create most of their work in the studio; not until the late 1860s, with the work of Claude Monet, Pierre-Auguste Renoir, and Camille Pissarro, the leaders of Impressionism, did painting *en plein air* become more popular. This change came about from 1881, when Monet, in his efforts to capture the true effects of light on the colour of landscape at any given moment, began to carry several canvases at once into the out-of-doors. On each he began a painting of the same subject at a different time of day; on subsequent days, he continued to work on each canvas in succession as the appropriate light appeared.

MINIATURE PAINTING

Miniature painting is a term applied both to Western portrait miniatures and to the Indian and Islamic forms of manuscript painting discussed below. Portrait miniatures, or limnings, were originally painted in watercolour with body colour on vellum and card. They were often worn in jeweled, enameled lockets. Sixteenth-century miniaturists, such as Hans Holbein the Younger, Jean Clouet, Nicholas Hilliard, and Isaac Oliver, painted them in the tradition of medieval illuminators. Their flat designs, richly textured and minutely detailed,

Nicholas Hilliard painted the watercolour miniature portrait *A Young Man Among Roses* c. 1588.

ROSALBA CARRIERA

The Venetian portrait painter and miniaturist Rosalba Carriera (1675–1757) was an originator of the Rococo style in France and Italy. She is best known for her work in pastels.

Some scholars suggest that Carriera learned lacemaking from her mother and that, as the lace industry declined, she instead began decorating snuffboxes for the tourist trade. Whatever the origins of her interest, Carriera first became known for her miniature portraits on snuffboxes. She was the first artist to use ivory rather than vellum as a ground for miniatures. By the time Carriera was age 25, her miniatures had won her special membership in the Academy of St. Luke in Rome.

Her art suited the refined taste of her times. Many notables passing through Venice commissioned portraits from her. The collector and financier Pierre Crozat encouraged her to go to Paris. She did so in March 1720, accompanied by her family, and became the idol of the French capital; she received commissions for 36 portraits, among them one of Louis XV as a child. She became a member of the French Royal Academy in 1720 and the next year returned to Venice and her home on the Grand Canal. In 1730 she once more left Venice, this time to work for six months in Vienna, where Holy Roman Emperor Charles VI became her patron and the empress became her pupil. After 1750 Carriera's sight failed.

often incorporated allegorical and gilded heraldic motifs. In 17th- and 18th-century Western portrait miniatures, the two-dimensional pattern of rich colours was developed by atmospheric tonal modeling into more naturalistic representations; these were sometimes in pastel and pencil or painted in oils on a metal base. Pantographs (reducing and enlarging copying instruments made on the lazy-tongs lever principle) might be used to transfer a drawing. Among the exponents of this naturalistic style were Francisco Goya, Fragonard, Samuel Cooper, and François Dumont. The introduction of painted ivory miniatures was followed, in the 19th century, by a decline in aesthetic standards, although a classical simplicity was achieved by unsophisticated itinerant limners and by the German miniaturist Patricius Kittner. The painted miniature was eventually superseded by the small, hand-tinted photograph.

MANUSCRIPT ILLUMINATION AND RELATED FORMS

Among the earliest surviving forms of manuscript painting are the papyrus rolls of the ancient Egyptian Book of the Dead, the scrolls of Classical Greece and Rome, Aztec pictorial maps, and Mayan and Chinese codices, or manuscript books. European illuminated manuscripts were painted in egg-white tempera on vellum and card. Their subjects included religious, historical, mythological, and allegorical narratives, medical treatises, psalters, and calendars depicting seasonal occupations. In contrast to the formalized imagery of Byzantine and early Gothic manuscript painters, Celtic illuminators developed a unique, abstract style of elaborate decoration, the written text being overwhelmed by intricate latticework borders, with full-page initial letters embraced by interlacing scrolls. The medieval Gothic style of illumination, in sinuous, linear patterns of flattened forms isolated against white or gilded grounds, had developed, by the end of the 15th century, into exquisitely detailed, jewel-like miniatures of shaded figures and spatial landscapes. These were often framed by gilded initial letters as vignettes or by margin borders in simulated half relief. With the advent of printing in the 15th century and a final, brilliant period of Flemish and Italian illumination, European manuscript painting survived only in official documents, maps, and in the form of hand-coloured, block-printed pages. Pennsylvanian-German birth and baptismal certificates in the United States and William Blake's hand-coloured engravings to the Bible and to his own poems were isolated revivals of those forms.

Indian and Islamic miniature painting, however, was practiced into the 19th century; and 11th-century Asian albums of poem paintings in ink, on leaves of silk or paper, represent a tradition that was continued into modern times. The subjects of Middle Eastern miniatures included religious and historical narrative, cosmic maps, and medical, palmistry, and astrological charts, as well as illustrations to poems, songs, and romantic epics. These were generally painted in gouache on paper, with occasional gold- or silver-leaf embellishment. The linear design was first drawn with a brush in delicate contours and soft shading. Landscape and architectural detail was as well observed as in that of the principal figures.

The first two letters of Christ's name in Greek, chi and rho, are depicted in the illuminated gospel book, the Book of Kells (c. 800). The artists used various pigments, such as indigo for blue and orpiment for yellow, on vellum.

The rapprochement established between text, painted borders, margin spaces, and illustration is characteristic of both Eastern and Western manuscript paintings. In Indian and Islamic miniatures, for example, the panels of decorative script are integrated within the overall pattern as areas of textural enrichment; and, with the margin and inset frames, these panels serve also as concrete screens and prosceniums to the action depicted, the participants in the narrative episode making their exits and entrances across or behind them.

SCROLL PAINTING

Hand scrolls, traditional to China and Japan, are ink paintings on continuous lengths of paper or silk. They are unrolled at arm's length and viewed from right to left. These generally represent panoramic views of rivers, mountain and urban landscapes, and domestic interiors. They also illustrate romantic novels, Daoist and Buddhist themes, and historical and genre subjects. Narrative poetic commentaries were included as integral textures in the flowing design. The scrolls are remarkable for their vitality, the lyrical representation of atmospheric space, and for the rising and dipping viewpoints that anticipate the zooming motion-picture camera. The earliest surviving scrolls, such as Gu Kaizhi's *The Admonitions of the Court Instructress*, date from the 4th century CE. Asian hanging scrolls and Indian and Tibetan temple banners are forms similar to those of Western easel and panel paintings. Their subjects range from the

The landscape painting *Minghuang's Journey to Shu*, ink and colour on a silk hanging scroll, is attributed to Li Zhaodao, Tang-dynasty style, possibly a 10th/11th-century copy of an 8th-century original.

seasons, domestic interiors, landscapes, and portraits to Vishnu epics, mandalas (symbolic diagrams of the universe), and temple icons. They are painted in ink or gouache on silk and paper and are usually mounted on embroidered or block-printed silk. The dramatic interplay of bold, flattened images against the open space of an unpainted or gilded ground influenced 19th-century Western Art Nouveau decoration.

CHINESE AND JAPANESE SCROLLS

Scroll painting was practiced primarily in East Asia. The two dominant types may be illustrated by the Chinese landscape scroll, which is that culture's greatest contribution to the history of painting, and the Japanese narrative scroll, which developed the storytelling potential of painting.

The earliest "illustrative" Chinese scrolls, forerunners of the narrative type, date from the late 4th century CE and teach Buddhist moral lessons. The continuous scroll form was fully developed by the 7th century. Such a scroll is opened from right to left and viewed on a table. The landscape hand scroll (*makimono*), a pictorial rather than narrative form, reached its greatest period in the 10th and 11th centuries with masters such as Xu Daoning and Fan Kuan. The viewer becomes a traveler in these paintings, which offer the experience of moving through space and time. There is frequent depiction of roads or paths that seem to lead the viewer's eye into the work.

Only about 2 feet (0.6 metre) of such a scroll should be viewed at one time or the spirit of the work is violated. One problem faced by the artists was a need for multiple vanishing points in generating a sense of perspective, since the imaginary viewer was assumed not to be stationary. They solved this in a variety of ways, causing one perspective point to fade unnoticed into the next.

Nearly contemporary with the Chinese panoramic landscapes are the Japanese *emakimono*, scroll paintings of the 12th and 13th centuries. These are long horizontal scrolls, 10–15 inches (25–38 cm) wide and up to 30 feet (9 metres) long. This painting tradition is called *Yamato*-e, or Japanese painting, to distinguish it from Japanese work in the Chinese manner. In the earliest example of this form, *The Tale of Genji*, Japan's great literary masterpiece, is shown in pictures alternating with text. Eventually the illustration in such works stood nearly alone, and typical subjects were the stories and biographies popular during Japan's Middle Ages. The Japanese taste for sensation and drama finds vivid expression in these scrolls. The buildings pictured in them are frequently without roofs, so that intimate interior scenes can be shown, and backgrounds are tilted forward so as to pack more incident into a smaller space.

During the renaissance of Chinese tradition that followed this period, an alcove intended for a picture or flower arrangement, the *tokonoma*, was introduced. Paintings were made vertical instead of horizontal in order to fit this space. These hanging *kakemono*, with their static compositions and contemplative themes, are more in the nature of Western paintings.

SCREEN AND FAN PAINTING

Folding screens and screen doors originated in China and Japan, probably during the 12th century (or possibly earlier), and screen painting continued as a traditional form into the 20th. They are in ink or gouache on plain or gilded paper and silk. Their vivid rendering of animals, birds, and flowers and their atmospheric landscapes brought nature indoors. In some screens each panel was designed as an individual painting, while in others a continuous pattern flowed freely across the divisions. Japanese screens were often painted in complementary yin and yang pairs. Large 12-panel Chinese coromandel lacquer screens were imported into Europe during the 17th and 18th centuries. French Rococo boudoir screens depicting *fêtes champêtres* (townspeople enjoying rural surroundings) and *toile de Jouy* (landscape or floral) pastoral themes were painted on silk or on wood panels in a flamboyantly scrolled, gilded framework. The designs of Art Nouveau screens were inspired by the Japanese tradition. Sidney Nolan's screens on Greek themes and the pastiches of Victorian paper-scrap screens by Pop art painters are recent Western revivals. Traditional to the Greek and Russian Orthodox churches is the iconostasis screen, which stands between the nave and sanctuary and displays icon panel paintings representing the Virgin, the saints, and narrative subjects.

Rigid fans are depicted in the paintings and reliefs of ancient Egypt, Assyria, Greece, and Rome, but the oldest surviving specimens are the round and folding fans from East Asia. These were painted in India ink and colour on paper, card, and silk, the ground often sprinkled with gold dust or laid with gold or silver leaf.

Spread freely across the mount, a calligraphic design depicted seasonal landscapes, genre scenes, and bird, flower, and animal motifs, with accompanying poems and commentaries. Leading Asian painters produced much of their finest work in this form. In Europe, however, where fan painting had been rarely practiced until the 17th century, it was considered a minor art, and designs were often based on frescoes and easel paintings. The richest and most elegant of these were painted in France and Italy during the 18th century. Watercolour and gouache paintings and hand-coloured engraved designs were made on paper, card, kid, and gauze. Allegories and romantic pastoral landscapes were frequently designed as separate vignettes, linked by floral swags and border scrolls. Both sides of the mount might be painted. The guards and sticks of the spoke framework were in delicately carved wood or ivory, inlaid with gold leaf or mother-of-pearl. Round hand-screens of parchment, mounted on handles like lollipops, were popular in early 19th-century English society. Charles Conder was a notable fin de siècle ("end of the century," characterized by effete sophistication) fan painter, and, in the early 20th century, Oskar Kokoschka decorated a lively set of fans on an autobiographical narrative theme.

PANORAMAS

Panoramas were intended to simulate the sensation of scanning an extensive urban or country view or seascape. This form of painting was popular at the end of the 18th century. Notable examples are *The Battle of Agincourt* (1805), by R.K. Porter, and the *Mesdag Panorama* (1881), by Hendrik Willem Mesdag. Panoramas might be compared to Cinerama films and enjoyed as a stimulating optical entertainment, along with cyclorama drums (large pictorial representations encircling the spectator), trompe l'oeil diorama peep shows, and the show box, for which Thomas Gainsborough painted glass transparencies. More serious forms of panoramic painting are exemplified in Chinese Buddhist sanctuary frescoes, Asian hand scrolls, Dürer's watercolour townscapes, Andrey Rublyov's 14th-century mural of Moscow, and Uccello's original sequence of three panels, about 1438–40, depicting the Battle of San Romano.

MODERN FORMS

The concept of painting as a medium for creating illusions of space, volume, texture, light, and movement on a flat, stationary support was challenged by many modern artists. Some late 20th-century forms, for example, blurred the conventional distinctions between the mediums of sculpture and painting. Sculptors such as David Smith, Eduardo Paolozzi, and Philip Sutton made multicoloured constructions; painters such as Jean Arp and Ben Nicholson created abstract designs in painted wood relief, and Richard Smith painted on three-dimensional canvas structures the surfaces of which curl and thrust toward the spectator. And, rather than deny the essential flatness of the painting support by using traditional methods of representing volume and texture, Robert Rauschenberg and Jim Dine attached real objects and textures to the painted surface, and Frank Stella and Kenneth Noland designed their irregularly shaped canvases to be seen as explicitly flat art objects. Rejecting earlier painting methods of reproducing effects of light with tonal contrasts and broken pigment colour, some artists made use of neon tubes and mirrors. Instead of simulating sensations of movement by optical illusion, others designed kinetic panels and boxes in which coloured shapes revolved under electric power. The traditional definition of painting as a visual, concrete art form was questioned by Conceptual art, in which the painter's idea might be expressed only in the form of documented proposals for unrealized and often unrealizable projects. In performance art and happenings, which employed techniques akin to those used in theatre, the artists themselves became a kind of medium.

THE CONSERVATION OF PAINTINGS

Broadly speaking, most paintings can be divided into (1) easel paintings, on either canvas or a solid support, usually wood; (2) wall, or mural, paintings; and (3) paintings on paper and ivory. The conservator of paintings aims above all at "true conservation," the preservation of the objects in conditions that, as far as possible, will arrest material decay and delay as long as possible the moment when restoration is needed. The correct choice of conditions of display and storage is, therefore, of the first importance. Ideally, each type of painting requires its own special conditions for maximum safety, depending on the original technique and materials used to compose it.

Portable paintings on canvas or panel are called easel paintings. Basically, they consist of the support (the canvas or panel); the ground, ordinarily a white or tinted pigment or inert substance mixed with either glue or oil; the paint itself, which is composed of pigments held in a binding medium such as drying oil, glue, egg, casein, or acrylic; and, finally, the surface coating, usually a varnish, to protect the paint and modify its appearance aesthetically. These four layers have many variants but must be constantly borne in mind when considering the problems of conservation.

PAINTINGS ON WOOD

Wood has been used as a support since the encaustic paintings of ancient Greece. Wood-panel supports were used almost universally in European art in devotional icons and other works before the 16th century, when the use of canvas became dominant. Wood has the disadvantage of swelling and shrinking across the grain when there are variations in the relative humidity of the atmosphere. In northern temperate climates, variations in humidity can be considerable. In England, for example, the seasonal variation in a museum that is centrally heated in the winter can be from 25 percent in midwinter to 90 percent in summer. Although paint has a certain elasticity, it cannot usually take up much movement, and in paintings on wood it generally cracks in a network referred to as "craquelure." In continental landmasses, such as the United States, the average relative humidity in dry zones may be consistently low, so that European paintings with wooden supports "air-seasoned," or accustomed, to a higher humidity may suffer considerably. In both Europe and the United States, the combination of an unsuitable environment of low or changing relative humidity with the restraining effect of the paint layer often produces a permanent bowing of the panel, which is convex at the front surface.

To counteract both the shrinkage and the bowing (especially the latter), restorers in the past placed wooden strips called battens, or more complex structures called cradles, across the back of the panel as constraints. This solution, however, often produced internal stresses that led to severe distortion of the front surface, cracking of the panel along the wood grain, and in some instances extensive damage to the paint. This form of intervention has been largely abandoned in favour of an environmental approach that places the emphasis on the maintenance of a stable environment that fosters preservation. The ideal conservation solution is a form of air conditioning in which the relative humidity is maintained as much as possible at what is generally agreed to be the most reasonable level—i.e., about 55 percent. It is normal by modern standards to accept as inevitable some permanent convex curvature.

When warping and cracking have already occurred or when the latter seems likely as a result of the mistaken application of secondary supports, such as cross battens, expert restoration treatment is required. In principle, this consists of removing the cross battens and applying a reinforcement to the back that imposes a uniform but gentle constraint over the whole surface. In the past, when the wood was badly worm-eaten or dimensionally unstable, the wooden support was occasionally removed from the paint and ground layers in the process known as "transfer." This was accomplished by temporarily adhering a substantial support of paper and, possibly, canvas to the front surface and then cutting away the wood on the back. An entirely new support, of either panel or canvas, was then adhered to the back, and the temporary facing was removed. This treatment is very rarely done today and is generally considered to be an extreme form of intervention.

PAINTINGS ON CANVAS

Painting on canvas became common in the 16th century and has been used largely in European and American painting traditions. A canvas support expands and contracts with variations in relative humidity, but the effect is not as drastic as with wood. Canvas, however, will deteriorate with age and acidic conditions and may be easily torn. In many cases, parts of the paint and ground will lift from the surface, a condition variously called "cleavage," "flaking," "blistering," or "scaling." The traditional method to address these problems is to rein-force the back of the canvas by attaching a new canvas to the old in a process called "lining," also referred to as "relining." A number of techniques and adhesives have been employed for lining, but with all methods there is a risk of altering the surface texture of the painting if the procedure is not carried out with the utmost care and skill. The most frequently used technique until the mid-20th century consisted of ironing a new canvas to the old, using an adhesive composed of a warm mix-ture of animal glue and a farinaceous paste, sometimes with the addition of a small proportion of plasticizer. This method, though less common today, is still used, especially in Italy and France. It has the advantage that the heat and moisture help to flatten raised ("cupped") paint and local deformations and tears in the canvas. Another method, introduced after the mid-19th cen-tury, uses a thermoplastic wax-resin mixture. Originally executed with heated irons as in the glue-paste method, it increased in popularity by the introduction, around 1950, of the so-called "vacuum hot table."

With this table, the two canvases are coated with molten adhesive (at about 160 °F [70 °C]) and joined together on an electrically heated metal plate. They are covered with a membrane, enabling the air between the two canvases to be evacuated with a pump through holes at the corners of the table; adhesion then occurs on cooling. Excessive vacuum pressure and heat can drastically alter a painting's texture. In addition, during this process, wax penetration can darken canvas and thin or porous paint layers. To overcome this latter defect, "heat-seal" adhesives were introduced in the late 1960s. Formulations containing synthetic resins, including polyvinyl acetate and, increasingly, an ethylene-vinyl acetate copolymer, are applied in solution or dispersion to the surfaces and, after drying, are adhered on the hot table. Ethylene-vinyl acetate copolymer adhesives are also available as dry, nonpenetrating films. More recently, cold-setting polymer dispersions in water have been introduced by using a low-pressure suction table, from which the water is removed through spaced perforations in the table surface with a powerful down-draft of air. Pressure-sensitive adhesives have also been introduced as lining adhesives but have not been widely adopted. Although all these methods are currently in use, the trend has been to move away from lining and wholesale treatments in general in favour of more refined, precise, and limited treatments that address condition problems in a more specific way.

The low-pressure suction table mentioned above and a smaller device used for localized treatment generally referred to as a "suction plate" have gained wide use at the turn of the 21st century. The more elaborate versions of this instrument are equipped with heating elements and humidification systems beneath the perforated table surface. These features make it possible to apply controlled humidity, heat, and gentle pressure to perform a variety of treatments, including tear realignment and repair, reduction of planar deformations, and the introduction of consolidating adhesives to reattach cleaving paint. The practice of edge lining (sometimes referred to as "strip lining"), which has been increasingly used as an alternative to overall lining, aims to reinforce weak and torn edges where the canvas is prone to give way. This treatment is often used in conjunction with local or overall treatments executed by using the suction table and suction plate.

In the past, paintings have occasionally been transferred from wood to canvas by a variant of the treatments described above. The reverse of this—i.e., attaching a painting on canvas to a stable rigid support (a process known as "marouflage")—is still sometimes done for various reasons.

The ground (i.e., the inert paint layer covering the support below the painting itself) can ordinarily be regarded for conservation purposes as part of the painting layers. Occasionally, the ground may lose its adhesion to either the support or the paint layers, or the ground may fracture internally, resulting in cleavage and paint loss.

The paint layers themselves are subject to a number of maladies as a result of natural decay, faulty original technique, unsuitable conditions, ill treatment, and improper earlier restorations. It must be remembered that, whereas housepaint usually has to be renewed every few years, the paint of easel paintings is required to survive indefinitely and may be already 600 years old. The most prevalent defect is cleavage. If the loss is not total, the paint can be secured, according to circumstances, with a dilute protein adhesive such as gelatin or sturgeon glue, a synthetic polymer, or a wax adhesive.

The paint is usually coaxed into place with an electrically heated spatula or a micro hot-air tool.

As painting materials became more readily available in commercial preparations in the 18th and 19th centuries, systematic methods of painting that were once passed from master to apprentice were replaced by greater individual experimentation, which in some cases led to faulty technique. Artists sometimes used too much oil, leading to ineradicable wrinkling, or they superimposed layers that dried at different rates, producing a wide craquelure as a result of unequal shrinkage, a phenomenon that occurred increasingly as the 19th century progressed because of the use of a brown pigment called "bitumen." Bituminous paints never dry completely, producing a surface effect resembling crocodile skin. These defects cannot be cured and can be visually ameliorated only by judicious retouching.

A notable defect arising from aging is the fading or changing of the original pigments by excessive light. Although this is more evident with thin-layer paintings, such as watercolours, it is also visible in oil paintings. The palette of the earlier painters was, in general, stable to light; however, some of the pigments used, notably the "lakes," which consisted of vegetable dyestuffs mordanted onto translucent inert materials, often faded easily. Copper resinate, a transparent green much used from the 15th to the 18th century, became a deep chocolate brown after prolonged exposure to light. After the discovery of synthetic dyestuffs in 1856, a further series of pigments were created, some of which were later discovered to fade rapidly. Unfortunately, it is impossible to restore the original colour, and in this case conservation, in its true sense of arresting decay, is important; i.e., to limit the light to the lowest possible

A LAKE

A lake is any of a class of pigments composed of organic dyes that have been rendered insoluble by interaction with a compound of a metal. The interaction may involve the precipitation of a salt in which the proportions of dye to metal are fixed, or it may be a less well-defined attraction between the dye and the surfaces of particles of the inorganic compound. Some lakes are prepared by a combination of both processes. Lakes considerably extend the range of colours available in the production of paints, cosmetics, and inks for printing and lithography.

Dyes of several chemical classes are made into lakes by techniques that vary according to the nature of the salt-forming groups in the dye molecule. Mordant dyes and acid dyes form insoluble salts with metal ions, such as those of calcium and aluminum. Basic dyes contain amino groups and form insoluble salts with inorganic metal-containing acids such as phosphotungstic or phosphomolybdic acids.

level consistent with adequate viewing—in practice about 15 lumens per square foot (15 foot-candles; 150 lux). Ultraviolet light, the most damaging kind of light, which comes from daylight and fluorescent fixtures, can and must be filtered out in order to avoid damage.

Almost every painting of any degree of antiquity will have losses and damages, and a painting of earlier than the 19th century in perfect condition will usually be an object of special interest. Before a more conscientious approach to restoration became general in the mid-20th century, areas of paintings that had a number of small losses were often—indeed, generally—entirely repainted. It was considered normal in any case to repaint not only losses or gravely damaged areas but also a wide area of surrounding original paint, often with materials that would visibly darken or fade with time. Large areas with significant detail missing were often repainted inventively in what was supposed to be the style of the original artist. It is customary nowadays to inpaint only the actual missing areas, matching carefully the artist's technique and paint texture. Some restorers adopt various methods of inpainting in which the surrounding original paint is not imitated completely. The inpainting is done in a colour or with a texture intended to eliminate the shock of seeing a completely lost area without actually deceiving the observer. The aim in inpainting is always to use pigments and mediums that do not change with time and might be easily removed in any future treatment. Various stable, modern resins are employed in place of oil paint to ease reversibility and to avoid discoloration. Exact imitation of the original entails close study of the painter's technique, especially the multilayer methods, since the successive layers, being partly translucent, contribute to the final visual effect.

Minute details of texture, brushstrokes, and craquelure must also be simulated.

A variety of natural resins, sometimes mixed with drying oil or other constituents, have been used to varnish paintings. Although the traditional use of varnish was partly to protect the paint from accidental damage and abrasion, its main purpose was aesthetic: to saturate and intensify the colours and to give the surface a unified appearance. Mastic and damar, the most commonly used natural resins, are subject to deterioration. Their chief limitations are that they become brittle, yellow, and less soluble with age. In most cases a discoloured varnish may be safely removed by using organic solvent mixtures or other cleaning agents, but the process is very delicate and may cause significant physical and aesthetic harm to the painting when it is done improperly. Some paintings exhibit a greater sensitivity to cleaning than others, and some varnishes may be unusually intractable owing to their formulation. In addition, many organic solvents are known to leach components of the medium from oil paint. For these reasons, cleaning should be carried out only by an experienced professional, and the frequency of the procedure should be kept to an absolute minimum.

When the varnish is in good condition but covered with grime, the conservator may, after close inspection, clean the surface with aqueous solutions of nonionic detergents or mild solvents. Choice of solvent mixture and mode of application has always depended on the skill and experience of the conservator, but modern scientific theory has clarified the procedures. Synthetic resins have been widely adopted for use as picture varnishes. They are chosen for chemical stability with regard to light and atmosphere so that they can eventually be removed by safe solvents and will not rapidly discolour or physically deteriorate. Acrylic copolymers and polycyclohexanones have been the most commonly used since the 1960s. The synthetic varnish resins may be broadly divided into two classes of high-molecular-weight and low-molecular-weight resins. The high-molecular-weight resins are judged by many conservators to lack the desirable aesthetic and handling characteristics that are found in natural resins. Low-molecular-weight resins approach the appearance and behaviour of natural resins more closely and are currently receiving more attention. Recently introduced varnishes based on hydrogenated hydrocarbon styrene and methyl styrene resin hold promise as substitutes for natural resins. Research continues, however, in order to find the "ideal" varnish, combining ease of application, chemical stability, and an acceptable aesthetic quality. Paintings that are varnished, contrary to the intention of the artist, can become permanently altered in appearance over time and become diminished in value. In the last quarter of the 19th century, certain artists, most notably the Impressionists and Post-Impressionists, began to eschew the use of varnish.

WALL PAINTINGS

Wall paintings are the oldest known form of painting, dating back to the prehistoric paintings in the Altamira cave in Spain and the Lascaux Grotto in France. In the last decades of the 20th century, the conservation and restoration treatment of two Renaissance masterpieces of wall painting, Michelangelo's frescoes in the Sistine Chapel (the Sistine Ceiling [1508–12] and the *Last*

Judgment [1534–1541]) in Vatican City and Leonardo da Vinci's *Last Supper* (1495–98) in Milan, drew the world's attention to the environmental and structural vulnerabilities of these treasures.

Commonly, large paintings placed into architectural niches are considered "mural paintings," even those stretched over stationary or expandable wooden bars in the manner of easel paintings. Strictly speaking, however, "wall paintings" are distinguished from other murals by virtue of being executed directly onto primary wall supports, which are typically plaster, concrete, masonry, or stone. Wall paintings are integral to architecture, in both a material and aesthetic sense. The conservation of wall paintings inevitably concerns not only the paintings themselves but also the larger context of adjacent building materials, building maintenance, use, and preservation. Depending upon their construction and the degree of involvement of the wall support, wall paintings' conservation and restoration needs may be closely allied to those typical of easel painting or to those of porous stone.

From the point of view of conservation, different types of wall paintings have features in common, though the techniques of restoration required for each can differ greatly in detail. In *buon'* ("true") fresco, pigments mixed only in water are painted directly onto a freshly prepared layer of damp lime plaster. Pigments are permanently bound to the plaster as a result of a chemical change, as the fresh lime becomes calcium carbonate upon drying. In fresco *secco* ("dry"), the artist applies paints to already dried plaster. The stability of these paintings depends upon the presence of a binding medium—such as egg, oil, gum, or glue—mixed with the pigments to adhere them adequately to the wall surface.

This type of painting is found in the wall paintings of ancient Egypt. In marouflage, a more modern variety of wall painting, paintings on canvas are mounted to the wall using an adhesive.

Chief among the hazards to all these types of wall paintings is excessive moisture. Damp may rise through the walls, originating at the level of ground contact and spreading upward. Prevention of rising damp is sometimes achieved by cutting into the wall beneath the mural and inserting a "damp course" of water-impermeable material or a high capillary tube that draws and deflects the harmful accumulation. These avenues of intervention are, however, often prohibitively expensive due to the complex engineering they require. If these approaches are not possible, amelioration of the problems may be achieved by reconfiguring drainage at the exterior of the building, and thereby reducing the overall quantity of available moisture. Damp may also come from the outside wall, where direct infiltration of rainwater may penetrate through the substrate to the face of the painting, evaporating at the paint surface. In this instance, localized building repairs or efforts to shield the exterior wall may attenuate the problem. Moisture may also result from condensation on a cold mural surface, a phenomenon common in churches, tombs, or buildings that are heated only intermittently or that are subject to excess ambient moisture generated by the respiration of crowds of visitors. More continuous and uniform heating of the wall may adjust this situation, provided that ambient air is not dried so rapidly that "efflorescence" (the formation of salts) occurs. Lastly, water damage caused by leaking roofs, clogged drainpipes, and faulty plumbing is easily stopped by repairing these systems. Conscientious maintenance is the best preventative treatment.

Damages to wall paintings due to moisture may include blanching, drip staining, and delamination of paint layers due to efflorescence. Crystallized salts may form above, below, or within the painted image, resulting in disintegration or obfuscation of the image and creating a salty "veil." The conservator must avoid coating the painting with a water-impermeable material, such as wax or resinous products, so that the damp can penetrate freely without meeting a barrier at the inner surface; when evaporative sites are blocked, moisture will move laterally, expanding areas of damage. Problems such as mold growth and mildew are secondary results from overly damp environments.

Another enemy of wall paintings is more insidious and also more pervasive. Due to the worldwide use of fossil fuels and automobile emissions, concentrations of sulfur dioxide in the atmosphere have markedly increased. In the presence of moisture, pollutants forming sulfuric acid can quickly erode the calcium-carbonate component of most cement- and lime-based wall paintings. This "acid-rain" effect converts calcium carbonate to calcium sulfate. The volume of the sulfate crystal is almost twice that of the original carbonate of the mural, which causes internal pressure within the pores of wall fabric that can lead to fracturing. Further, the sulfate has a greater capacity to absorb moisture, thus perpetuating and exacerbating the cyclic wet-dry process of decay. Polluted environments can bring about the blackened, sooty surfaces associated with fossil-fuel particulates to a wall painting and can also discolour certain pigments traditionally found in Renaissance paintings, such as white or red lead, malachite, and azurite.

In the face of such damage from moisture and pollution, the conservator works to halt the causative agents of deterioration and then proceeds to stabilize insecurities such as spalling plaster or flaking paint. Many new conservation treatments were developed in the second half of the 20th century: chemical poultices, gel technology, and ion-exchange resins have allowed advances in cleaning methods, reduction of salt deposits, and consolidation techniques. Natural or synthetic adhesives and inorganic consolidants are now utilized, but they must be chosen for compatibility with the paint medium and used with discretion to avoid film-forming blockages. Hypodermic injection of adhesives followed by light pressure while drying has also become an effective way to mitigate many problems of detached paint or wall support.

Conservators often develop solutions in the face of a specific problem. For example, after the flood of the Arno River in Florence in 1966, Italian conservators developed drastic but necessary and highly expert methods to transfer frescoes from decayed walls. These range from the *strappo* technique to the *stacco a massello*. While in practice these methods are not always clearly distinguishable, *strappo*, the more radical procedure, consists of gluing canvas firmly to the surface of the fresco and then pulling and easing away a thin layer of the plaster containing the pigment particles of the fresco. The bond between the facing and the fresco must be stronger than the internal cohesion of the plaster. Excess plaster is removed from the back, revealing the thinned fresco in reverse. This thinned pictorial layer is then fixed to a rigid support after recoating the reverse with materials optically simulating the original underlying plaster. Unfortunately, much of the original surface character of the wall and density of the pigment layer is sometimes irreversibly altered by this technique, so the method is now seldom used. Less intrusive is the *stacco* method; a thicker layer of plaster is retained along with the fresco and is smoothed flat on its back surface before the composite rigid layer is mounted to a prepared support. Lastly, in the procedure called *stacco a massello*, the least intrusive to the fresco but more challenging transfer procedure due to mass and weight, the wall painting is removed with its entire original substrate. This feat requires bracing the wall with counter-forms to avoid damages due to torque, vibration, and other mechanical strains. Selecting the method of transfer depends greatly on the stability of the painting, the type of deterioration encountered, and the limitations of size, weight, and practicality.

Whenever possible, transfer techniques are abandoned in favour of conservation and restoration treatments carried out in situ, with the conservator working from the surface and preserving as much original building fabric, character of surface, and contextual meaning as possible. The art conservation community, including art historians and preservation specialists, generally hold that murals and wall paintings are physically and aesthetically dependent upon their architectural context. The so-called "site-specific" nature of the paintings is valued, and the character of the original site is maintained as nearly as possible; relocation may cause diminishment of meaning or appreciation. The disciplines of wall and mural painting conservation, engineering, and architectural conservation are symbiotic, and each specialty is increasingly called upon to contribute to a holistic preservation plan.

PAINTINGS ON IVORY

Ivory came into popular use as a painting support in the 18th and 19th centuries as part of miniature-painting traditions based largely in Europe and the United States. The naturally translucent material was well suited to the luminous techniques of portrait painting. Derived from the tusks and large teeth of elephants, walruses, and whales, ivory is composed of both organic and inorganic constituents of dentine. However, its porous and hygroscopic qualities render it vulnerable to many agents of deterioration. Ivory, especially in thin layers, responds with dimensional changes to fluctuations in the moisture content of the air. Miniature paintings on ivory are particularly vulnerable, expanding and contracting across the grain in a manner similar to paintings on wood. The conservation of ivory paintings depends to a large extent upon maintaining stable environmental controls, in the optimum region of 50–60 percent relative humidity, with the temperature not exceeding 70 °F (21 °C). At lower levels of relative humidity, paintings on ivory desiccate, shrink, and crack, especially if constrained. Relative humidity above about 68 percent promotes expansion and warping; cyclical fluctuations also place severe stresses on the paint media.

Light is another damaging agent and can be responsible for bleaching ivory surfaces. Watercolour and gouache, the most common painting media used in ivory miniatures, are sensitive to light and particularly subject to fading. Ideally, lighting of these objects should not exceed 5–10 lumens per square foot (5–10 foot-candles; 50–100 lux), and daylight should be avoided as much as possible. Since it is a porous sub- stance, ivory is susceptible to staining and to retaining unwanted oils; the use of cleaning agents, especially aqueous solutions, can result in damage and removal of patina. It is therefore advisable to wear gloves while handling these objects, and while in storage, ivory paintings should come in contact with only neutral pH materials such as soft cotton, linen, or unbuffered acid- free tissue.

PAINTINGS ON PAPER

Whereas paintings on parchment, vellum, papyrus, and bark in various forms date back to ancient times, it was not until after the invention of paper by the Chinese in the 2nd century CE that thin, felted cellulose sheets of true paper were available, mostly for calligraphic or printing uses. After the very slow progression of papermaking technology to the West, the first papers introduced for drawing or painting during Renaissance times were used as working sketches for paintings, sculptures, or architecture, rather than as completed artworks in themselves. During the Industrial Revolution, manufacturers created heavy paper sheets and lami- nated paperboards specifically for painting; having the mechanical properties requisite for full-colour illustration with pastel, gouache, oil, acrylic, or other paint media, these papers can clearly be considered apart from papers traditionally used for prints and drawings.

Depending upon the method of fabrication of the painting on paper, the design layer itself or the support may be the feature most responsible for an object's condition and for the response of the artwork to its environment. For instance, a thin sketch on lightweight paper, which has a great quantity of exposed paper as part of the image, is quite different in appearance and behaviour than a finished, opaque oil painting on heavy laminated paperboard, which may reveal none of the paper surface in its design. In the former case, the object may respond to its environment more characteristically like a print or drawing, whereas, in the latter case, the object may respond characteristically like a painting on wood or canvas. In this respect, paintings on paper may vary widely, and conservation requirements may fall generally into the category of either paper or painting. Conservation treatment is usually best addressed by the professional whose expertise is in the field of the dominant material.

Paintings on paper require the same environmental protections of most organic materials, namely, stable temperature and relative humidity within the limited range recommended (50–55 percent RH, 60–68 °F [16–20 °C]). Prolonged light exposure inevitably causes loss of colour and distortion of the artist's original concept or intention. A darkened paper support, combined with fading colorants, may seriously skew intentional contrasts and result in much loss of depth or detail. The conservator should avoid daylight exposure as much as possible, because the ultraviolet light component is particularly damaging. Ultraviolet filters over windows or incorporated into Plexiglas framing may be of some benefit in controlling light exposure, but these efforts are not a panacea and should not be used in place of prudent monitoring. The total quantity of light should be considered, based upon time and intensity, because damage due to light is both cumulative and irreversible. Storage or framing should always require use of 100 percent acid-free (preferably all rag) matte boards and storage folders in order to limit the chance of acidic transfer to the artwork. The humidity and ventilation of storage facilities should also be carefully monitored so as to avoid mold growth on sizing (the glue used in the binding process) and paint media, as well as to prevent secondary infestation by silverfish or book lice.

IMAGERY AND SUBJECT MATTER

The imagery and subject matter of paintings in early cultures were generally prescribed by tribal, religious, or dynastic authorities. In some Eastern countries, traditional models survived into the 18th century and even later. With the Renaissance, however, images and themes in Western painting, reflecting the new spirit of humanistic, objective curiosity and scientific research, came to be decided by the artist and his patron and, in later periods, by the artist alone.

KINDS OF IMAGERY

Within the various cultures the art of representing things by painted images has rarely shown a continuously developing pattern toward greater realism. More often, religious and philosophical precepts have determined the degree of naturalism permitted. Rules governing portrayals of the human figure have been particularly stringent in certain traditions of representational painting, reflecting different attitudes to the cosmic significance of humans. For example, a belief

in human inferiority in relation to an almighty deity
is expressed in the faceless figures of early Jewish
painting and in the stylizations of Byzantine imagery; and human insignificance against the dynamic
forces of nature is symbolized in Chinese landscape
paintings by man's puny scale within a monumental
setting. An earlier view, which instead sought to glo-
rify the spiritual, intellectual, and physical attributes of
humankind, is typified in the noble figures of Greco-
Roman art and in the renewed celebration of human
physical beauty in the Renaissance and subsequent
Neoclassical styles. The uniqueness of humans
among living things and the expression of individual
physical and emotional characteristics are exemplified in Japanese and northern European narrative
and genre painting. Concomitant with the antipathy
toward figurative representation in some cultures was
a general distaste for the portrayal of all things of the
exterior world, animals, landscape features, and other
natural forms rarely appearing except as stylized
images signifying spiritual forces of good and evil.
The representational imagery of modern painting bor-
rows freely from ancient and contemporary sources
such as untrained and child art, Classical mythology, commercial advertising, press photography, and
the allegories and fantasies of the motion picture
and the comic strip. Nonrepresentational imagery is
not restricted to modern painting but appears also
in earlier forms such as Aurignacian (Paleolithic)
decorative meanders, the scrollwork of Celtic illumi-
nations, and the patterns of Islamic Kūfic calligraphy
(an angular variety of the Arabic alphabet). And the
abstraction of natural forms into rudimentary symbols, characteristic of modern painting, is echoed in

the "pin-men" conventions of Magdalenian caves, in Aztec pictograms, and Indian and Tibetan cosmic-diagram paintings.

KINDS OF SUBJECT MATTER

Devotional, narrative, portraiture, genre, landscape, still life, animals and birds, and abstracts are many of the kinds of subject matter painters have included in their works.

DEVOTIONAL

The range and interpretation of subjects in different forms of devotional painting express a particular attitude to the relationship between man and God. Early Christian and Buddhist murals, for example, portrayed an all-powerful, remote, and mysterious being, painted as a flat, formalized head or figure whose stern gaze dominated the interiors of temples, churches, and sanctuaries. Christian Last Judgments and Buddhist hell paintings were intended to frighten believers, while subjects such as the Virgin enthroned, the Assumption, and Buddha descending from Paradise sustained their faith with hopes for salvation and rewards of blissful immortality.

NARRATIVE

When the autocratic ecclesiastical control over Western painting weakened under Renaissance humanism, the religious narrative picture became a window onto a terrestrial rather than a celestial world. Both emotional and physical relationships between the figures depicted were realistically expressed, and the spectator was able to identify himself with the lifelike representation of a worldly space inhabited by Christ, his disciples, and saints, wearing updated dress and moving naturally within contemporary settings. This kind of narrative interpretation persists in the modern religious paintings of Sir Stanley Spencer, where biblical environments are represented by the clipped hedgerows, the churchyards, and the front parlours of his neat, native English village of Cookham.

Allegorical narrative subjects might exalt the sensuous arts, as in the symbolic muses portrayed by Poussin and Luca Signorelli and the paradisiac gardens of 15th-century French illuminated manuscripts. But they might also carry warnings. In the 16th century, Pieter Bruegel the Elder, for example, combined overt and often grotesque symbols with subtle visual metaphors to point stern morals in such paintings as *The Triumph of Death* ([c. 1562], alluding to the "wages of sin"), *The Land of Cockaigne* ([1567], attacking gluttony and sloth), and *Mad Meg* ([1562], ridiculing covetousness). Even Bruegel's apparently straightforward genre subjects, such as *The Peasant Dance* (c. 1568) and the festival of *The Fight Between Carnival and Lent* (1559), conceal parables on human folly and sin, while Hiëronymus Bosch introduced abstruse, allegorical phantasmagoria into such traditional narratives as *The Temptation of St. Anthony* (c. 1500) and *The Prodigal Son* (c. 1510) and made his *Garden of Earthly Delights* (c.1505–10)

Hiëronymus Bosch painted the dreamlike *Garden of Earthly Delights* (c. 1505–10) as a triptych. The allegorical narrative shows the earthly paradise with the creation of woman, the first temptation, and the Fall.

an expression of disgust rather than of joy. Botticelli's late paintings, probably produced under the influence of the 15th-century Italian monk and reformer Girolamo Savonarola, are other savagely pessimistic allegories: *The Story of Virginia Romana* (c. 1500) and *The Tragedy of Lucretia* (c. 1499), representing virtue upheld only by death, and *The Calumny of Apelles* (c. 1495), in which envy, suspicion, deceit, guile, repentance, and truth are identified, like medieval mummers, by their costume, pose, and gesture. Rubens, however, found in allegorical symbolism a means of dramatizing mundane state commissions, such as *The Union of Scotland and Ireland* (c. 1632–34) and *The Bounty of James I* (*Triumphing over Avarice*) (1632–33). Among famous 19th-century allegories are Delacroix's *Liberty*

SHĀH-NĀMEH

A celebrated work by the Persian epic poet Firdawsi, the *Shāh-nāmeh* ("Book of Kings") is the composition in which the Persian national epic found its final and enduring form. Completed in about 1010 and dedicated to Sultan Mahmūd of Ghazna, the work was based mainly on the *Khvatay-nāmak*, a Pahlavi (Middle Persian) prose history of the kings of Persia. Firdawsi versified and updated the story to the time of the downfall of the Sassanid empire in the mid-7th century. Comprising nearly 60,000 short rhyming couplets, the *Shāh-nāmeh* has remained one of the most popular works in the Persian-speaking world. Its episodes have inspired miniaturists from the 14th century to the present, and numerous attempts have been made to emulate it in Iran, India, and Turkey.

The work deals with Persian history from its mythical beginnings to historical events, including the acceptance of the Zoroastrian faith, Alexander the Great's invasion, and the conquest of the country by the Arabs. A large part of the work centres on tales of the hero Rostam. The struggle between Persia and Turan (the central Asian steppes from which new waves of nomadic conquerors distributed Persian urban culture) forms the central theme, and the importance of the legitimate succession of kings, who are endowed with royal charisma, is reflected throughout the composition.

Leading the People (1830) and Pierre-Paul Prud'hon's *Justice and Divine Vengeance Pursuing Crime* (1808).

Possibly the highest achievements in narrative illustrations to poetry and literature are found in Eastern miniatures and Asian scrolls, such as the Persian paintings of Ferdowsī's 11th-century national epic poem, the *Shāh-nāmeh*, and the 12th-century Japanese scrolls of the *Genji monogatari* and the *Story of Ben Dainagon*. An example of modern literary painting is Sir Sidney Nolan's narrative series (1946–47) portraying the Australian folklore hero Ned Kelly.

Ancient Greek and Roman mythologies have provided Western artists with rich sources of imagery and subject matter and with opportunities for painting the nude. Historical narrative painting includes Classical mythology and heroic legend, as well as the representation of contemporary events; examples include Benjamin West's *Death of Wolfe* (c. 1771), Théodore Géricault's *Raft of the Medusa* (c. 1819), and Goya's *The 3rd of May in Madrid* (1808).

PORTRAITURE

The earliest surviving portraits of particular persons are probably the serene, idealized faces painted on the front and inside surfaces of dynastic Egyptian sarcophagi. The human individuality of the Roman mummy portraits of the 1st and 2nd century CE, however, suggests more authentic likenesses. Although portraits are among the highest achievements in painting, the subject poses special problems for the artist commissioned to paint a notable contemporary. The portraits of patrons by artists such as Raphael, Rubens, Hyacinthe Rigaud, Antoine-Jean Gros, Jacques-Louis David, and Sir Thomas Lawrence were required to express nobility, grace, and authority, just as the sultans and rajahs portrayed on frontispieces to Persian and Indian illuminated books and albums had understandably to be flattered as benevolent despots. Such concessions to the sitter's vanity and social position seem to have been disregarded, however, in the convincing likenesses by more objective realists such as Robert Campin, Dürer, Jan van Eyck, Velázquez, Goya, and Gustave Courbet. Probably the finest are the self-portraits and studies of ordinary people by Rembrandt and van Gogh, where psychological insight, emotional empathy, and aesthetic values are fused. A more decorative approach to the subject is seen in the flattened portraits by Holbein, the Elizabethan and itinerant naïve American limners of the Colonial era, and the East Asian paintings of ancestors, poets, priests, and emperors. Like these paintings, the full-length portraits by François Boucher, Gainsborough, Kees van Dongen, and Matisse display as much regard for the texture and form of their sitters' dress as for their facial features.

Photography changed the practice of portraiture in painting for much of the 20th century, except where artists such as Cézanne and Braque used it as a subject for structural research or—like Amedeo Modigliani, Chaim Soutine, and Francis Bacon—for the expression of a personal vision beyond the scope of the camera. In roughly the last third of the 20th century, however, a number of painters, including Lucian Freud, Leon Kossoff, Francesco Clemente, Chuck Close, and Alex Katz, again took up portraiture.

REMBRANDT VAN RIJN AND PORTRAITS

Rembrandt van Rijn (1606–1669) was a Dutch Baroque painter and printmaker, one of the greatest storytellers in the history of art, possessing an exceptional ability to render people in their various moods and dramatic guises. Rembrandt is also known as a painter of light and shade and as an artist who favoured an uncompromising realism that would lead some critics to claim that he preferred ugliness to beauty.

Early in his career and for some time, Rembrandt painted mainly portraits. Although he continued to paint–and etch and, occasionally, draw–portraits throughout his career, he did so less frequently over time. Roughly one-tenth of his painted and etched oeuvre consists of studies of his own face as well as more-formal self-portraits, a fact that has led to much speculation.

The core of Rembrandt's oeuvre, however, consists of biblical and–to a much lesser extent–historical, mythological, and allegorical "history pieces," all of which he painted, etched, or sketched in pen and ink or chalk. Seen over his whole career, the changes in Rembrandt's style are remarkable. His approach to composition and his rendering of space and light–like his handling of contour, form, and colour, his brushwork, and (in his drawings and etchings) his treatment of line and tone–are subject to gradual (or sometimes abrupt) transformation, even within a single work. The painting known as *The Night Watch* (1640/42) was clearly a turning point in his stylistic development. These changes are not the result of an involuntary evolution; rather they should be seen as documenting a conscious search in pictorial and narrative respects, sometimes in discussion, as it were, with his great predecessors.

Rembrandt's massive group portrait *The Company of Frans Banning Cocq and Willem van Ruytenburch* (1642), better known as *The Night Watch*, is an oil painting on canvas.

(*CONTINUED ON THE NEXT PAGE*)

(*CONTINUED FROM THE PREVIOUS PAGE*)

Rembrandt quickly achieved renown among Dutch art lovers and an art-buying public for his history paintings and etchings, as well as his portraits and self-portraits. His unusual etchings brought him international fame during his lifetime, and his drawings, which in fact were done as practice exercises or as studies for other works, were also collected by contemporary art lovers.

In 1631 Rembrandt entered a business relationship with Hendrick Uylenburgh (1584 or 1589–c. 1660), an Amsterdam entrepreneur in paintings who had a large workshop that painted portraits, carried out restorations, and produced copies, among other activities.

From 1631 to 1635, in Uylenburgh's workshop, Rembrandt produced a substantial number of portraits (mainly pairs of pendants) and some group portraits, such as *The Anatomy Lesson of Dr. Nicolaes Tulp* (1632). He must have conquered the Amsterdam portrait market rapidly. Partly relying on his experience as a history painter, he succeeded in producing much livelier portraits than those created by the specialized portrait painters who had dominated the Amsterdam scene before his arrival. By limiting the amount of detail and using simple but dynamic contours, Rembrandt avoided distracting the viewer's attention. He led the eye primarily to the face and the suggested movement of the figure. He was also exceptionally good at rendering human skin convincingly.

There is doubt, however, about Rembrandt's ability to capture the likeness of his sitters. Constantijn Huygens, a Dutch diplomat, intellectual, and art connoisseur who discussed Rembrandt in an autobiography about his youth, wrote some epigrammatic Latin verses occasioned by a portrait of one of his friends that Rembrandt had painted in 1632. In these verses he wittily mocked the inadequacy of the portrait's likeness. The doubt that Rembrandt's portraiture was accurate is only exacerbated when one compares his authentic self-portraits with one another. The physiognomic differences between these images are considerable. In cases where it is possible to compare a portrait by Rembrandt with portraits of the same model by other painters, one has the impression that the likeness produced by Rembrandt was the least accurate. This seems to be the case, for instance, in his portrait of the famous banned Remonstrant preacher Johannes Wtenbogaert (1577–1644).

Stylistic analysis of his portraits reveals that Rembrandt occasionally had others assist him to a varying degree in the painting of portraits, as indeed was the custom in many portrait studios. For example, Wtenbogaert's portrait session with Rembrandt is recorded in a written document; back in Holland for some weeks, the preacher

(CONTINUED ON THE NEXT PAGE)

(*CONTINUED FROM THE PREVIOUS PAGE*)

recorded in his diary that on April 13, 1633, he posed for Rembrandt during only that one day. Parts of this portrait, such as the preacher's hands, were clearly painted by a studio assistant, no doubt after the sitter had left the studio.

In a number of his self-portraits, Rembrandt is wearing various types of antiquated dress. These costumes have been identified as allusions to great predecessors. For instance, the 16th-century northern European costume he is wearing in his famous 1640 self-portrait presumably referred to Albrecht Dürer, a fellow great *peintre-graveur* whom Rembrandt greatly admired and tried to emulate.

The 1640 self-portrait belongs to a category of paintings that could be termed trompe l'oeil works. With these paintings viewers are momentarily deceived by the sensation that they are in the same space as the painting's subject, forgetting that they are looking at a flat surface and subsequently experiencing the pleasure of this deception. Among Rembrandt's paintings from the period 1639–42, there are also still lifes with dead birds, portraits, and group portraits that use trompe l'oeil tricks. Some of his pupils of that period, including Samuel van Hoogstraten, Fabritius, and Rembrandt's German pupil, Christoph Paudiss (1630–66), continued to exploit trompe l'oeil effects.

In 1640–42 Rembrandt must have been occupied mainly with the large group portrait depicting members of an Amsterdam civic militia company.

In his painting of this scene, which later would acquire the name *The Night Watch*, Rembrandt revolutionized the formula of the group portrait as part of his continuing effort to achieve the ultimate liveliness in his work. In the words of van Hoogstraten, Rembrandt's former pupil, "Rembrandt made the portraits that were commissioned subservient to the image as a whole."

Van Hoogstraten, who had praised the unity in *The Night Watch's* composition, criticized his former master by complaining, "I would have preferred if he [Rembrandt] would have kindled more light into it." Van Hoogstraten's remarks were published in his book on the art of painting. His notes on the subordination of the portraits to the conception as a whole, and the lack of light in the painting, have contributed to the myth of *The Night Watch* being rejected and of Rembrandt's subsequent "fall."

In the decade following 1642, Rembrandt's production changed in several ways. His output of paintings diminished drastically, and the few paintings he made varied in subject, size, and style. Moreover, he produced no painted portraits, a fact that can be interpreted in two ways: either he did not receive any portrait commissions during that period or he did not accept such commissions for the decade. At the same time, he embarked on a number of extremely

(*CONTINUED ON THE NEXT PAGE*)

(CONTINUED FROM THE PREVIOUS PAGE)

ambitious etchings, such as the portrait (1647) of his friend Jan Six (1618–1700) and especially the *Hundred Guilder Print*, a large (unfinished) print with episodes from chapter 19 of The Gospel According to Matthew.

In his later years (1658–69), Rembrandt received commissions for portraits, among which a group portrait of the sampling officials of the Amsterdam Drapers' Guild (*The Syndics of the Amsterdam Drapers' Guild*, 1662), an anonymous family group (mid-1660s), and an anonymous *Portrait historié as Isaac and Rebecca* (1667), better known as *The Jewish Bride (portrait historié* is a phrase used to indicate a portrait in which the sitter is–or in this case the sitters are–rendered in a historic role with historicizing costumes).

GENRE

Genre subjects are scenes from everyday life. Hunting expeditions and tribal rituals figure in prehistoric rock paintings. Domestic and agricultural occupations, with banquet scenes of feasting, dancing, and music, were traditional subjects for ancient Egyptian tomb murals. East Asian hand scrolls, albums, and screens brilliantly describe court ceremonies, the bustle of towns, and the hardships of the countryside. The depiction of earthly pursuits was forbidden under the strict iconography prescribed by the early Christian Church, but the later illuminated Books of Hours provide enchanting records of the festivals and occupations of northern European communities. In Renaissance painting, genre subjects were generally restricted to background features of portraits and historical narratives. Domestic scenes, however, not only provided Bruegel with subjects for moral allegories but, as with Rembrandt, were used to counterpoint the emotional intensity of a dramatic religious theme. The withdrawal of religious patronage in northern Europe directed painters toward secular subjects. The rich period of genre painting in the 17th-century Netherlands is represented by the interiors, conversation pieces, and scenes of work and play by David Teniers the Younger, Frans Hals, Jan Steen, Judith Leyster, Gerard Terborch, Pieter de Hooch, Adriaen van Ostade, and, the finest, by Johannes Vermeer.

Pictures of rustic life had a special appeal for collectors in 18th-century France and England; these were the somewhat picturesque representations of peasant life painted by Jean-Baptiste Greuze, Boucher, George Morland, and Gainsborough. Jean-Baptiste-Siméon Chardin's paintings of servants and children, however, exhibit a timeless dignity and grandeur. The harsher realities of working life were depicted by

Johannes Vermeer depicts everyday life in *Woman Holding a Balance* (c. 1664), and evokes abstract moral and philosophical ideas.

JOHANNES VERMEER

Johannes Vermeer (1632–1675) was a Dutch artist who created paintings that are among the most beloved and revered images in the history of art. Although only about 36 of his paintings survive, these rare works are among the greatest treasures in the world's finest museums. Vermeer began his career in the early 1650s by painting large-scale biblical and mythological scenes, but most of his later paintings–the ones for which he is most famous–depict scenes of daily life in interior settings. These works are remarkable for their purity of light and form, qualities that convey a serene, timeless sense of dignity. Vermeer also painted cityscapes and allegorical scenes.

Surprisingly little is known about Vermeer's decision to become a painter. He registered as a master painter in the Delft Guild of Saint Luke on December 29, 1653, but the identity of his master(s), the nature of his training, and the period of his apprenticeship remain a mystery.

Since Vermeer's name is not mentioned in Delft archival records during the late 1640s or early 1650s, it is possible that, as with many aspiring Dutch artists, he traveled to Italy, France, or Flanders. He also may have trained in some other artistic centre in the Netherlands, perhaps Utrecht or Amsterdam. In Utrecht Vermeer would have met artists who were immersed in the boldly expressive traditions of Caravaggio, among them Gerrit van Honthorst. In Amsterdam he would have encountered the impact of Rembrandt van Rijn, whose powerful chiaroscuro effects enhanced the psychological intensity of his paintings.

Stylistic characteristics of both pictorial traditions—the Utrecht school and that of Rembrandt—are found in Vermeer's early large-scale biblical and mythological paintings, such as *Diana and Her Companions* (1655–56) and *Christ in the House of Mary and Martha* (c. 1655). The most striking assimilation of the two traditions is apparent in Vermeer's *The Procuress* (1656). The subject of this scene of mercenary love is derived from a painting by the Utrecht-school artist Dirck van Baburen in the collection of Vermeer's mother-in-law, while the deep reds and yellows and the strong chiaroscuro effects are reminiscent of Rembrandt's style of painting. The dimly lit figure at the left of the composition is probably a self-portrait in which Vermeer assumes the guise of the Prodigal Son, a role that Rembrandt had also played in one of his own "merry company" scenes.

In the early 1650s Vermeer might also have found much inspiration back within his native Delft, where art was undergoing a rapid transformation. The most important artist in Delft at the time was Leonard Bramer, who produced not

(*CONTINUED ON THE NEXT PAGE*)

(CONTINUED FROM THE PREVIOUS PAGE)

only small-scale history paintings–that is, morally edifying depictions of biblical or mythological subjects–but also large murals for the court of the Prince of Orange. Documents indicate that Bramer, who was Catholic, served as a witness for Vermeer at his marriage. Although it would appear that Bramer was, at the very least, an early advocate for the young artist, nowhere is it stated that he was Vermeer's teacher.

Another important painter who Vermeer must have known in Delft during this period was Carel Fabritius, a former Rembrandt pupil. Fabritius's evocatively pensive images and innovative use of perspective seem to have profoundly influenced Vermeer.

Whatever the circumstances of his early artistic education, by the second half of the 1650s Vermeer began to depict scenes of daily life. These "genre" paintings are those with which he is most often associated.

Vermeer's interior scenes during this period were also influenced by the work of Pieter de Hooch, a leading genre painter in Delft at the time. De Hooch was a master of using perspective to create a light-filled interior or courtyard scene in which figures are comfortably situated. Although no documents link Vermeer and de Hooch, it is highly probable that the two artists were in close contact during this period, since the subject matter and style of their paintings during those years were quite similar. Vermeer's *The Little Street* (c. 1657–58) is one such work: as with de Hooch's courtyard scenes, Vermeer has here portrayed a world of domestic tranquillity, where women and children go about their daily lives within the reassuring setting of their homes.

During the height of his career, in paintings depicting women reading or writing letters, playing musical instruments, or adorning themselves with jewelry, Vermeer sought ways to express a sense of inner harmony within everyday life, primarily in the confines of a private chamber. In paintings such as *Young Woman with a Water Pitcher* (c. 1664–65), *Woman with a Pearl Necklace* (c. 1664), and *Woman in Blue Reading a Letter* (c. 1663–64), he utilized the laws of perspective and the placement of individual objects—chairs, tables, walls, maps, window frames—to create a sense of nature's underlying order. Vermeer's carefully chosen objects are never placed randomly; their positions, proportions, colours, and textures work in concert with his figures. Radiant light plays across these images, further binding the elements together.

Although he drew his inspiration from his observations of everyday life in such mature work, Vermeer remained at his core a history painter, seeking to evoke abstract moral and philosophical ideas. This quality is particularly evident in *Woman Holding a Balance* (c. 1664). In this remarkable

(*CONTINUED ON THE NEXT PAGE*)

(*CONTINUED FROM THE PREVIOUS PAGE*)

image, a woman stands serenely before a table that bears a jewelry box draped with strands of gold and pearls while she waits for her small handheld balance to come to rest. Although the subdued light entering the room and the refined textures of the jewelry and fur-trimmed jacket are realistically rendered, the painting of the Last Judgment hanging on the rear wall signifies that the artist conceived the scene allegorically. As the woman stands by the jewelry box and Judgment scene, her calm expression indicates a realization: she must maintain balance in her own life by not allowing transient worldly treasures to outweigh lasting spiritual concerns.

Perhaps the most recognizable feature of Vermeer's greatest paintings is their luminosity. Technical examinations have demonstrated that Vermeer generally applied a gray or ochre ground layer over his canvas or panel support to establish the colour harmonies of his composition. He was keenly aware of the optical effects of colour, and he created translucent effects by applying thin glazes over these ground layers or over the opaque paint layers defining his forms. His works further seem to be permeated with a sense of light as a result of his use of small dots of unmodulated colour—as in the aforementioned buildings and water of *View of Delft*, and in foreground objects in other works, such as the crusty bread in *The Milkmaid* (1658–60) and the finials of the chair in *Girl with the Red Hat* (1665–66).

The diffuse highlights Vermeer achieved are comparable to those seen in a camera obscura, a fascinating optical device that operates much like a box camera. The 17th-century camera obscura created an image by allowing light rays to enter a box through a small opening that was some-times fitted with a focusing tube and lens. Owing to the device's limited depth of field, the image it projected would have many unfocused areas surrounded by hazy highlights. Vermeer was apparently fascinated by these optical effects, and he exploited them to give his paintings a greater sense of immediacy.

Some have argued that Vermeer used the device to plan his compositions and even that he traced the images projected onto the ground glass at the back of the camera obscura. However, such a working process is most unlikely. Vermeer instead relied primarily on traditional perspective constructions to create his sense of space. It has been discovered, for example, that small pinholes exist in many of his interior genre scenes at the vanishing point of his perspective system. Strings attached to the pin would have guided him in constructing the orthogonal lines that would have defined the recession of floors, windows, and walls. Vermeer carefully placed this vanishing point to emphasize the main compositional element in the painting. In *Woman Holding a Balance*, for example, it occurs at the fingertip of the hand

(CONTINUED ON THE NEXT PAGE)

holding the balance, thus enhancing his overall philosophical message. Such attention to detail helps explain the small size of Vermeer's creative output, even during his most fertile period. He must have worked slowly, carefully thinking through the character of his composition and the manner in which he wanted to execute it.

Jean-François Millet, Daumier, Courbet, van Gogh, and Degas; the robust gaiety of cafés and music halls was captured by Henri de Toulouse-Lautrec, John Sloan, Everett Shinn, and Walter Richard Sickert; and intimate domestic scenes were recorded by Bonnard and Vuillard. Modern genre movements have included the American Scene painters, the Ashcan and Kitchen Sink schools (represented by such painters as George Wesley Bellows, Jack Smith, and Derrick Greaves), the Camden Town and Euston Road groups (Frederick Spencer Gore, Sir William Coldstream, and Victor Pasmore), and the Social Realists in England and in the United States (Robert Henri, Stuart Davis, and Maurice Prendergast).

LANDSCAPE

Idealized landscapes were common subjects for fresco decoration in Roman villas. Landscape painting (as exemplified by a Chinese landscape scroll by Gu Kaizhi dating from the 4th century) was an established tradition in East Asia, where themes such as the seasons

Albrecht Dürer's watercolour *The Monumental Turf* (1503) represents one of the earliest pure landscape works.

CLAUDE LORRAIN

French artist Claude Lorrain (1600–82) was among the greatest masters of ideal land-scape painting, an art form that presented nature as more beautiful and harmonious than it really was. Ideal landscapes often show classical ruins and pastoral people in classical dress, using the countryside around Rome as inspiration. Claude's special contribution was the poetic rendering of light.

Claude Lorrain, who is usually called Claude in English, was born Claude Gellée, or Gelée, in 1600, in the village of Chamagne, Lorraine (France). His parents were poor, and they apparently died when he was 12 years old. Within a few years he traveled south to Rome, Italy. There he was trained as an art-ist by the Italian landscape painter Agostino Tassi. Tassi taught Claude the basic subjects of his art–landscapes and coast scenes with buildings and little figures–and gave him a lasting interest in perspective.

In 1625 Claude went back to Nancy, the capital of Lorraine, where he worked for a year as an assistant on some frescoes in the Carmelite church. But, in the winter of 1626–27, Claude returned to Rome and set-tled there permanently. Little is known of his personality. He lived essentially for his work. Although his schooling was limited, the subjects of his paintings show that he had an adequate knowledge of the Bible, Ovid's *Metamorphoses*, and Virgil's *Aeneid*. Keenly sought after as an artist, he pursued a successful career into old age and amassed a comfortable fortune.

Claude's first surviving dated work is *Landscape with Cattle and Peasants* (1629). In the early 1630s he rose to fame, partly because of two or three series of landscape frescoes. By about 1637 he had become the leading landscape painter in Italy. Claude's early works, influenced by Tassi and by Dutch and Flemish artists, are busy, animated, and picturesque.

At the same time, Claude began painting seaports, which were idealized harbor scenes. Light is the key feature of these seaport pictures. Its source is often a visible sun just above the horizon, which Claude first introduced in 1634 in *Harbor Scene*–it was the first time an artist used the sun to illuminate a whole picture. He further emphasized this subtle sense of perspective by painting outlines and colours that were gradually less distinct from the foreground to the background.

Beginning about 1640 Claude began to make his compositions more classical and

(*CONTINUED ON THE NEXT PAGE*)

(CONTINUED FROM THE PREVIOUS PAGE)

monumental. The influence of contemporary Bolognese landscape painting, particularly the works of Domenichino, replaces that of Tassi and the northern Europeans. The light is clearer than in paintings of Claude's early or late periods. Spacious, tranquil compositions are drenched in an even light, as can be seen in *Landscape: The Marriage of Isaac and Rebekah* (also called *The Mill*; 1648).

Claude's paintings of the 1650s, such as *The Sermon on the Mount*, are even larger and more heroic. In the middle of the 1660s his style moved into its last phase, when some of his greatest masterpieces were produced. The colour range is restricted, and the tones become cool and silvery. The paintings of this period are solemn and mysterious. It was in this spirit that Claude painted his famous work *The Enchanted Castle* (1664).

About 250 paintings by Claude, out of a total of perhaps 300, and more than 1,000 drawings have survived. He also produced 44 etchings. His paintings influenced a number of Dutch painters who were in Rome during the late 1630s and '40s.

and the elements held a spiritual significance. In Europe, imaginary landscapes decorated 15th-century Books of Hours. The first naturalistic landscapes were painted by Dürer and Bruegel. Landscapes appeared in most Renaissance paintings, however, only as settings to portraits and figure compositions. It was not until the 17th-century Dutch and Flemish schools—of Rembrandt, Jacob van Ruisdael, Meindert Hobbema, Aelbert Cuyp, Peter Paul Rubens, and Hercules Seghers—that they were accepted in the West as independent subjects. The most significant developments in 19th-century painting, however, were made through the landscapes of the Impressionists and the Neo-Impressionists and Post-Impressionists. Styles in landscape painting range from the tranquil, classically idealized world of Poussin and Claude, the precise, canal topography of Francesco Guardi and Canaletto and the structural analyses of Cézanne to the poetic romanticism of Samuel Palmer and the later Constables and Turners and the exultant pantheism of Rubens and van Gogh. Modern landscapes vary in approach from the Expressionism of Oskar Kokoschka's cities and rivers, Maurice de Vlaminck's wintry countrysides, and John Marin's crystalline seascapes to the metaphysical country of Max Ernst, Salvador Dalí, and René Magritte and the semi-abstract coastlines of Nicolas de Stael, Maria Elena Vieira da Silva, and Richard Diebenkorn.

STILL LIFE

The earliest European still-life painting is usually attributed to Jacopo de' Barbari (i.e., *Dead Bird*, 1504).

Vincent van Gogh's still life *Sunflowers* (1888) illustrates the Dutch painter's spontaneous and instinctive style of heavy applications of paint and exudes energy and light.

In Western paintings, still life often appears as a minor feature of the design; but until the 17th century it was not generally painted for its own sake, although it was already traditional to East Asian art. The subject

WILLIAM HARNETT

William Harnett (1848–1892) was an American still-life painter who was one of the masters of trompe l'oeil painting in the 19th century.

As a child, Harnett was brought to Philadelphia, where he later trained as an engraver and studied at the Pennsylvania Academy of the Fine Arts. His early work shows the influence of the Philadelphia still-life artists Raphaelle and James Peale. In 1880 he went to Europe, visiting London, Frankfurt, Munich, and finally Paris, where he painted his best-known work, *After the Hunt* (1885). He returned to the United States in 1886 and, except for another European trip in 1889, lived in New York City until his death. Among his favourite subjects were firearms (*The Faithful Colt*, 1890), books (*Job Lot, Cheap*, 1878), and musical instruments (*The Old Violin*, 1886).

Harnett's paintings were extremely popular with the public, but most critics thought his works were mere trickery. Both groups ignored his outstanding skill in abstract composition. After a long period of disrepute, Harnett's works again were appreciated and sought after in the mid-20th century.

is particularly associated with northern European painting, and the choice of objects very often has a religious or literary significance: wine, water, and bread symbolizing the Passion; skulls, hourglasses, and candles, the transience of life; and selected flowers and fruits, the seasons. Flower painting, especially, held a spiritual and emotional meaning for Japanese artists and for 19th-century European painters, such as Odilon Redon, Paul Gauguin, and van Gogh. Still life has been expressed in many different ways: Giuseppe Arcimboldo's witty arrangements of fruit, flowers, and vegetables made into fantastic allegorical heads and figures; the sensuous representation of food by Frans Snyders, Goya, and William Merritt Chase; the trompe l'oeil illusionism of Alexandre-François Desportes and William Harnett; the formal decoration of folk artists or untrained artists such as Henri Rousseau and Séraphine and of modern painters such as Matisse, Raoul Dufy, and Pat Caulfield; the semi-abstract designs of Picasso, Juan Gris, and William Scott; and, probably at its highest level of expression, the majestic still lifes of Chardin, Cézanne, and Giorgio Morandi.

OTHER SUBJECTS

Since ancient times, animals and birds have provided the primary subject matter of a painting or have been included in a design for their symbolic importance. In the paintings of prehistoric caves and dynastic Egyptian tombs, for example, animals are portrayed with a higher degree of naturalism than human figures. Their texture, movement, and structure have provided some artists with a primary source of inspiration: the classical, anatomical grace of a George Stubbs racehorse and a more romantic interpretation in the ferocious energy of a Rubens and Géricault stallion; the vivid expression of rhythmically co-ordinated movements of deer by Tawaraya Sotatsu and Antonio Pisanello; the weight and volume of George Morland's pigs and Paul Potter's cows; the humanized creatures of Gothic bestiaries and of Edward Hicks's *Peaceable Kingdom* (c. 1833–34); and, finally, Dürer's *The Hare* (1502), which is possibly as famous as Leonardo's *Mona Lisa* (c. 1503–06).

Increasing interest is shown in notable painters' versions of other artists' works. These are not academic copies (such as the study made by Matisse, when a student, of Chardin's *La Raie*) but creative transcriptions. Examples that can be appreciated as original paintings are those by Miró of Hendrik Sorgh's *Lute Player*; by Watteau of Rubens's *Apotheosis of James I*; by Degas of Bellini's *Jealous Husband*; by Caulfield of Delacroix's *Greece Expiring on the Ruins of Missolonghi*; by Larry Rivers of Jean-Auguste-Dominique Ingres's *Mlle Rivière*; and by Picasso of Manet's *Déjeuner sur l'herbe*, Velázquez's *Las Meñinas*, and Delacroix's *Woman of Algiers* (which produced Roy Lichtenstein's *Femmes d'Alger, After Picasso, After Delacroix*). Picasso has also painted free versions of works by El Greco, Lucas Cranach, Poussin, and Courbet, as Rubens had of Mantegna and Titian, Rembrandt of Persian and Indian miniatures, Cézanne of Rubens and El Greco, and van Gogh of Millet, Gustave Doré, and Delacroix.

In an abstract painting, ideas, emotions, and visual sensations are communicated solely through lines, shapes, colours, and textures that have no representational significance. The subject of an abstract painting

ABSTRACT EXPRESSIONISM

Abstract Expressionism was a broad movement in American painting that began in the late 1940s and became a dominant trend in Western painting during the 1950s. The most prominent American Abstract Expressionist painters were Jackson Pollock, Willem de Kooning, Franz Kline, and Mark Rothko. Others included Clyfford Still, Philip Guston, Helen Frankenthaler, Barnett Newman, Adolph Gottlieb, Robert Motherwell, Lee Krasner, Bradley Walker Tomlin, William Baziotes, Ad Reinhardt, Richard Pousette-Dart, Elaine de Kooning, and Jack Tworkov. Most of these artists worked, lived, or exhibited in New York City.

Although it is the accepted designation, Abstract Expressionism is not an accurate description of the body of work created by these artists. Indeed, the movement comprised many different painterly styles varying in both technique and quality of expression. Despite this variety, Abstract Expressionist paintings share several broad characteristics. They are basically abstract–i.e., they depict forms not drawn from the visible world. They emphasize free, spontaneous, and personal emotional expression, and they exercise considerable freedom of technique and execution to attain this goal, with a particular emphasis laid on the exploitation of the variable physical character of paint to evoke expressive qualities (e.g., sensuousness, dynamism, violence, mystery, lyricism). They show similar emphasis on the unstudied and intuitive application of that paint in a form of psychic improvisation akin to the automatism of the Surrealists, with a similar intent of expressing the force of the creative unconscious in art. They display the abandonment of conventionally structured composition built up out of discrete and segregable elements and their replacement with a single unified, undifferentiated field, network, or other image that exists in unstructured space. And finally, the paintings fill large canvases to give these aforementioned visual effects both monumentality and engrossing power.

The early Abstract Expressionists had two notable forerunners: Arshile Gorky, who painted suggestive biomorphic shapes using a free, delicately linear, and liquid paint application; and Hans Hofmann, who used dynamic and strongly textured brushwork in abstract but conventionally composed works. Another important influence on nascent Abstract Expressionism was the arrival on American shores in the late 1930s and early '40s of a host of Surrealists and other important European avant-garde artists who were fleeing Nazi-dominated Europe. Such artists greatly stimulated the native New York City painters and gave them a more intimate

(CONTINUED ON THE NEXT PAGE)

(CONTINUED FROM THE PREVIOUS PAGE)

view of the vanguard of European painting. The Abstract Expressionist movement itself is generally regarded as having begun with the paintings done by Jackson Pollock and Willem de Kooning in the late 1940s and early '50s.

In spite of the diversity of the Abstract Expressionist movement, three general approaches can be distinguished. One, Action painting, is characterized by a loose, rapid, dynamic, or forceful handling of paint in sweeping or slashing brushstrokes and in techniques partially dictated by chance, such as dripping or spilling the paint directly onto the canvas. Pollock first practiced Action painting by dripping commercial paints on raw canvas to build up complex and tangled skeins of paint into exciting and suggestive linear patterns. De Kooning used extremely vigorous and expressive brushstrokes to build up richly coloured and textured images. Kline used powerful, sweeping black strokes on a white canvas to create starkly monumental forms.

The middle ground within Abstract Expressionism is represented by several varied styles, ranging from the more lyrical, delicate imagery and fluid shapes in paintings by Guston and Frankenthaler to the more clearly structured, forceful, almost calligraphic pictures of Motherwell and Gottlieb.

The third and least emotionally expressive approach was that of Rothko, Newman, and

Reinhardt. These painters used large areas, or fields, of flat colour and thin, diaphanous paint to achieve quiet, subtle, almost meditative effects. The outstanding colour-field painter was Rothko, most of whose works consist of large-scale combinations of soft-edged, solidly coloured rectangular areas that tend to shimmer and resonate.

Abstract Expressionism had a great impact on both the American and European art scenes during the 1950s. Indeed, the movement marked the shift of the creative centre of modern painting from Paris to New York City in the postwar decades. In the course of the 1950s, the movement's younger followers increasingly followed the lead of the colour-field painters and, by 1960, its participants had generally drifted away from the highly charged expressiveness of the Action painters.

may be therefore a proposition about the creative painting process itself or exclusively about the formal elements of painting, demonstrating the behaviour of juxtaposed colours and shapes and the movements and tensions between them, their optical metamorphosis and spatial ambiguities. Many abstracts, however, are more than visual formal exercises and produce physical and emotional reactions in the spectator to illusions of shapes and colours that appear to rise and fall, recede and advance, balance and float, disintegrate and re-form; or of moods created of joy, sadness, peace, or foreboding; or of effects produced by light or by flickering or throbbing movement. Some abstracts evoke the atmosphere of a particular time, place, or event; and then their titles may be significant: *Pancho Villa, Dead and Alive* (Robert Motherwell); *Late Morning* (Bridget Riley); *Broadway Boogie Woogie* (Piet Mondrian); *Gold of Venice* (Lucio Fontana); *Capricious Forms* (Wassily Kandinsky).

SYMBOLISM

Most early cultures developed iconographic systems that included prescriptions for the site, design, function, form, medium, subject matter, and imagery of their painting.

DEVOTIONAL ICONOGRAPHY AND FORM

The siting of early Byzantine murals, for instance, echoed the symbolic, architectural planning of the basilica. Thus, a stylized, linear image of Christ, surrounded by heavenly hosts, occupied the central dome; the Virgin was represented in the apse; and stiff figures of apostles, prophets, martyrs, and patriarchs occupied the aisle walls. The format of early devotional paintings was also prescribed, Christian and Buddhist deities being placed in the focal centre of the design, above the eye level of the audience and larger than surrounding figures. And, in the conventional arrangement of a Christian subject such as the Holy Trinity, a central, bearded, patriarchal God, flanked by archangels, presented Christ on the

Tintoretto's *The Trinity* (1564), oil on canvas, is an example of a traditional arrangement of the Christian subject and its symbolism.

cross; between them was a dove, representing the Holy Spirit. In a rendering of the risen Christ, the Son faced the audience, with the Virgin Mother on the left and St. John on the right of the design. In East Asia a traditional format depicted Buddha on a lotus throne or in a high chariot drawn by oxen across clouds, surrounded by figures representing the planets. Deities generally appear against undefined grounds of white (signifying eternity or nothingness), blue (the celestial vaults), or gold (representing heavenly light by radiating lines or the spiritual aura by a nimbus). The elaborate surface preparation of supports and the painstaking execution with the finest materials symbolized the intention that paintings dedicated to a deity should last forever. The imagery, subject matter, and form might also have a mystical function: the realistic rendering of animals in contrast to the perfunctory human representations in Ice Age rock paintings, thought to signify a wishful guarantee for success in hunting; the earthly pleasures depicted on ancient Egyptian tomb murals intended to secure their continuance for the deceased; and the North American Indian sand paintings designed for magic healing ceremonies and the Tantric (relating to Tantrism, a school of Mahayana Buddhism) mandalas used for meditation and enlightenment.

SYMBOLISM IN EASTERN PAINTING

The symbolism in Eastern painting—intended to deepen the experience of a picture's mood and spirituality—is more generalized and poetic than in Western art. Both the execution and the subject matter of Buddhist Chinese and Japanese painting have a religious or metaphysical significance: the artist's intuitive, calligraphic brush movements symbolizing his mystical empathy with nature and his cyclic landscape and flower subjects expressing his belief in the spiritual harmony of natural forms and forces. Much of Indian symbolism is visually emotive, images such as snakes, plantain leaves, twining creepers, and rippling water being overtly sexual. And, although symbolic attributes and colour codes identify Indian mythological characters (for example, the four arms of the terrible goddess Kali and the blue skin of the divine lover Krishna), the formal character and colour scheme of settings generally

KALI

In Hinduism, Kali is the goddess of time, doomsday, and death, or the black goddess (the feminine form of Sanskrit *kala*, "time-doomsday-death" or "black"). Kali's origins can be traced to the deities of the village, tribal, and mountain cultures of South Asia who were gradually appropriated and transformed, if never quite tamed, by the Sanskritic traditions. She makes her first major appearance in Sanskrit culture in the *Devi Mahatmya* ("The Glorifications of the Goddess," c. 6th century CE). Kali's iconography, cult, and mythology commonly associate her not only with death but also with sexuality, violence, and, paradoxically, in some later traditions, with motherly love.

Although depicted in many forms throughout South Asia (and now much of the world), Kali is most often characterized as black or blue, partially or completely naked, with a long lolling tongue, multiple arms, a skirt or girdle of human arms, a necklace of decapitated heads, and a decapitated head in one of her hands. She is often portrayed standing or dancing on her husband, the god Shiva, who lies prostrate beneath her. Many of those portrayals depict her sticking out her tongue, which is sometimes said to indicate her surprise and embarrassment at discovering that she is trampling on her husband. Yet the association of Kali with an extended tongue has early roots. A precursor of Kali is the ogress Long Tongue, who licks up oblations in the ancient Sanskrit texts known as the Brahmanas. The *Devi Mahatmya* tells of Kali springing from the anger of the goddess Durga to slay the demon Raktabija ("Blood-Seed"). During the struggle a new demon emerges from each drop of Raktabija's blood as it hits the ground; to prevent this, Kali laps up the blood before it can reach the ground. She is also said to have been born when the goddess Parvati shed her dark skin; the sheath became Kali—who is also called Kaushika, "The Sheath"–leaving Parvati in the form of Gauri ("The Fair One").

Worshipped throughout India but particularly in Kashmir, Kerala, South India, Bengal, and Assam, Kali is both geographically and culturally marginal. Since the late 20th century, feminist scholars and writers in the United States have seen Kali as a symbol of feminine empowerment, while members of New Age movements have found theologically and sexually liberating inspiration in her more violent sexual manifestations.

Krishna Lifting Mount Govardhana is an example of Mewār miniature painting from the early 18th century.

reflect the narrative's emotional mood (for example, vibrant, dark-blue, cloudy skies and embracing, purple-black glades evoking amorous anticipation and red grounds expressing the passions of love or war).

SYMBOLISM IN WESTERN PAINTING

Western symbolic systems, however, are more intellectually directed, their imagery having precise literary meanings and their colour codes intended primarily for narrative or devotional identification. The iconographic programs of the early Christian churches, for example, laid down complex formulas for the viewpoints, gestures, facial expressions, and positions of arms, hands, and feet for religious figures. An elaborate Ethiopian Christian iconographic system was followed until very recently, and elsewhere traditional methods survive of identifying archangels and saints by their attributes and by the symbols of martyrdom that they display: distinguishing white-bearded St. Peter from black-bearded St. Paul, for example, and portraying St. Catherine with a wheel and St. Bartholomew with a knife and skin. Christian iconography adopted and elaborated Greco-Roman and Jewish symbolic imagery: the pagan signs of the vine and the fish, for example, and the image of Christ as the Good Shepherd based on the Greek Hermes Kriophoros. Medieval and Renaissance writings define an immense vocabulary of symbolic images, such as the crescent, sea urchin, and owl signifying heresy, the toad and jug representing the devil, and the egg and bagpipes as erotic symbols (all of which appear in Hiëronymus Bosch's 15th-century narrative moralities). Angels and devils, hellfire and golden paradise, heavenly skies and birds in flight representing spirituality and rebirth are examples of the similarity of symbolic meaning for many religious, mythological, and allegorical traditions. The significance of images common to several cultures, however, may also be very different: the dragon representing avarice in European medieval allegory symbolizes friendliness in Japanese Zen painting; and the snake, symbol of temptation and eroticism in the West, signifies, by its skin shedding, the renewal of life in East Asian iconography.

It is through the fine art of painting that the artist expresses ideas and emotions, as well as a version of the reality he or she perceives, in a two-dimensional visual form. The language of the artist consists of shapes, lines, colours, tone, and textures that are blended in various ways to produce in the viewer sensations of light, space, and movement. Some artists paint concrete forms with which viewers are generally familiar. Others try to create entirely abstract relationships. To study the paintings of any age is to look in on the diverse interpretations of the era in which they were produced.

Modern art embraces a wide variety of movements, theories, and attitudes whose modernism resides particularly in a tendency to reject traditional, historical, or academic forms and conventions in an effort to create an art more in keeping with changed social, economic, and intellectual conditions.

The beginnings of modern painting cannot be clearly demarcated, but there is general agreement that it started in 19th-century France. The paintings of Gustave Courbet, Édouard Manet, and the Impressionists represent a deepening rejection of the prevailing academic tradition and a quest for a more naturalistic representation of the visual world. These painters' Post-Impressionist successors can be viewed as more clearly modern in their repudiation of traditional techniques and subject matter and their expression of a more subjective personal vision. From about the 1890s on, a succession of varied movements and styles arose that are the core of modern art and that represent one of the high points of Western visual culture. These modern movements include Neo-Impressionism, Symbolism, Fauvism, Cubism, Futurism, Expressionism, Suprematism, Constructivism, Metaphysical painting, De Stijl, Dada, Surrealism, Social Realism, Abstract Expressionism, Pop art, Op art, Minimalism, and Neo-Expressionism. Despite the enormous variety seen in these movements, most of them are characteristically modern in their investigation of the potentials inherent within the painting medium itself for expressing a spiritual response to the changed conditions of life in the 20th century and beyond. These conditions include accelerated technological change, the expansion of scientific knowledge and understanding, the seeming irrelevance of some traditional sources of value and belief, and an expanding awareness of non-Western cultures.

Painting in the 21st century has been influenced by cultural globalization, a phenomenon by which the experience of everyday life, as influenced by the diffusion of commodities and ideas, reflects a standardization of cultural expressions around the world. Propelled by the efficiency or appeal of wireless communications, electronic commerce, popular culture, and international travel, globalization has been seen as a trend toward homogeneity that will eventually make human experience everywhere essentially the same. This appears, however, to be an overstatement of the phenomenon. Although homogenizing influences do indeed exist, they are far from creating anything akin to a single world culture.

With the development of Internet art and digital painting, artists are investigating new creative possibilities in which they can use virtual canvases and a computer's graphic software to produce virtual

Digital artists use virtual canvases and computer software with various paint tools to create their works. Many still use traditional paint chips as well.

paintings using a virtual paint box with digital brushes and other tools. The digital computer can create forms and shapes that did not exist previously. Digital painters can undo brush strokes and edit images effortlessly. They can mix palettes, apply layers, and add light effects, surfaces, and details to create unique pictorial concepts. In the contemporary art world the market for digital art is growing along with an increasing number of digital art exhibitions and the flourishing of online auction houses.

The almost unlimited global access that people today have to reproductions of artwork online and to the websites of historical collections has significantly broadened the understanding of painting throughout its history, artists' techniques, styles, and applications or practices. Active participation by amateurs in the act of painting helps individuals explore the meaning of their experiences. By giving expression to personal feelings, the artist develops individuality. An appreciation of painting deepens and enriches life.

Abstract art Also called nonobjective art or nonrepresentational art, painting, sculpture, or graphic art in which the portrayal of things from the visible world plays no part.

abstruse Hard to understand.

acrylic paint Paint that has pigments in a solution of acrylic resin.

acrylic resin A glassy plastic made especially from acrylic acid and used to cast and molded parts or as coatings and adhesives.

Action painting Direct, instinctual, and highly dynamic kind of art that involves the spontaneous application of vigorous, sweeping brushstrokes and the chance effects of dripping and spilling paint onto the canvas.

aesthetics A pleasing appearance or effect: beauty. A branch of philosophy that studies and explains the principles and forms of beauty especially in art and literature.

alla prima A method of painting in which pigments are laid on in a single application instead of being built up by repeated paintings.

allegory The written, oral, or artistic expression by means of symbolic fictional figures and actions of truths or generalizations about human conduct or experience.

assemblage An artistic composition made by putting together scraps or junk.

atmospheric perspective Also called aerial perspective, the expression of space in painting by gradation of colour or distinctness; the diminution of clarity of outline and intensity of colour in a distant object as distance increases: the optical effect produced by diffusion of light whereby objects appear lighter in tone the farther away they are viewed.

Barbizon school Mid-19th-century French school of painting, part of a larger European movement toward naturalism in art.

blanching Destructive of colour.

chromatic Of or relating to colour or colour phenomena or sensations.

commission An order to perform a particular task or carry out a work.

Conceptual art An art form in which the artist's intent is to convey a concept rather than to create an art object.

distemper A process of painting in which the pigments are mixed with an emulsion of egg yolk, with size, or with white of egg, or when distinguished from tempera with size only as a vehicle and usually used for scene painting or the decoration of usually plaster walls and ceilings. Also, the paint or the prepared ground used in the distemper process of painting.

efflorescence The process of changing on the surface or throughout to a whitish mealy or crystalline powder from the loss of water of crystallization on exposure to the air; formation of salts.

farinaceous Having a mealy texture or surface.

fixative Something that stabilizes or sets: as a varnish used especially for the protection of pencil, charcoal, or pastel drawings.

foreshortening To shorten (a detail) in a drawing or painting so that the composition appears to have depth.

hue The attribute of colours that permits them to be classed as red, yellow, green, blue, or an intermediate between any neighbouring pair of these colours; gradation of colour.

impasto The thick application of a pigment to a canvas or panel in painting.

limner An illuminator of medieval manuscripts; one that draws or paints, especially a self-taught itinerant artist.

linseed oil A yellowish drying oil obtained from flaxseed and used especially in paint, varnish, printing ink, and linoleum.

marouflage A process of fastening canvas to a wall with an adhesive (as white lead ground in oil).

mastic A yellowish to greenish resin of a small southern European tree used in varnish; a pasty material used as a protective coating or cement.

ochre An earthy usually red or yellow and often impure iron ore used as a pigment; the colour of yellow ochre.

palette A thin board or tablet on which a painter mixes pigments; the set of colours put on the palette; a particular range, quality, or use of colour.

panorama In the visual arts, continuous narrative scene or landscape painted to conform to a flat or curved background, which surrounds or is unrolled before the viewer.

patronage The support or influence of a patron; a benefactor's provision.

permutate Change or interchange; especially, to arrange in a different order.

perspective The art or technique of painting or drawing a scene so that objects in it have apparent depth and distance.

phantasmagoria An optical effect by which figures on a screen appear to dwindle into the distance or to rush toward the observer with enormous increase of size; a scene that constantly changes or fluctuates.

physionotrace A device used in the late 18th and early 19th centuries to trace the profile of a sitter with chalk or white crayon on a red paper, the image being then completed in black or white crayon.

pictograph An ancient or prehistoric drawing or painting on a rock wall; one of the symbols belonging to a system of picture writing.

primeval Primitive; of or relating to the earliest ages.

rapprochement Establishment of a state of having cordial relations.

resin Any of various solid or semisolid fusible natural organic substances that are usually transparent or translucent and yellowish to brown, are formed especially in plant secretions, are soluble in organic solvents but not in water, are electrical nonconductors, and are used chiefly in varnishes, printing inks, plastics, and sizes and in medicine.

Salon A fashionable gathering of notables customarily held at the home of a prominent person; a place for the exhibition of art.

scale A think layer, coating, or incrustation forming especially on metal.

sinuous Of serpentine or wavy form: winding.

size A gluey material (as a preparation of glue, flour, varnish, or resins) used for filling the pores in a surface (as of paper, textiles, leather, or plaster), as a stiffener (as of fabric), or as an adhesive for applying colour or metal leaf to book edges or covers. In oil painting it is crucial that the canvas be coated with the size so that its absorbency is reduced and contact with the paint is avoided.

tempera A process of painting in which the colours are mixed with substances (as egg, glue, or gum) other than oil.

trompe l'oeil A style of painting in which things are painted in a way that makes them look like real objects.

turpentine An essential oil obtained from oleoresins that are derived from coniferous trees by distillation and used especially as a solvent and thinner.

vellum A fine-grained lambskin, kidskin, or calfskin prepared especially for writing on or for binding books; a strong cream-coloured paper resembling vellum.

GENERAL WORKS ON PAINTING

Both Kimberley Reynolds with Richard Seddon, *Illustrated Dictionary of Art Terms* (1981, reissued 1984); and Ralph Mayer, *A Dictionary of Art Terms and Techniques* (1969, reissued 1981), include modern art references. Two works by Harold Osborne (ed.), *The Oxford Companion to Art* (1970), and *The Oxford Companion to Twentieth-Century Art* (1981), provide extensive bibliographies. Also see René Huyghe (general ed.), *Larousse Encyclopedia of Prehistoric and Ancient Art*, rev. ed. (1966, reissued 1981); *Larousse Encyclopedia of Byzantine and Medieval Art*, rev. ed. (1966, reissued 1981); *Larousse Encyclopedia of Renaissance and Baroque Art* (1964, reissued 1981); and *Larousse Encyclopedia of Modern Art* (1965, reissued 1981).

Design: Good surveys of the subject include Frederick Malins, *Understanding Paintings: The Elements of Composition* (1981); and Johannes Itten, *Design and Form: The Basic Course at the Bauhaus*, rev. ed. (1975; originally published in German, 1963). Works on colour include Josef Albers, *The Interaction of Color* (1963, reissued with rev. plate section, 1975); Johannes Itten, *The Art of Color* (1961, reissued 1973; originally published in German, 1961); Faber Birren, *Creative Color* (1961), and (ed.), *A Grammar of Color: A Basic Treatise on the Color System by Albert H. Munsell* (1969); Robert L. Herbert, *Neo-Impressionism* (1968); William Innes Homer, *Seurat* and the Science of Painting (1964, reprinted 1978); and Barbara Rose, "The Primacy of Color," *Art International*, 8:22–26 (1964). The influence of photography on painting is examined in Aaron Scharf, *Art and Photography* (1968, reissued 1974); and Karen Tsujimoto, *Images of America: Precisionist Painting and Modern Photography* (1982).

Mediums: Standard works on most painting materials, supports, surfaces, and techniques include Ralph Mayer, *The Artist's Handbook of Materials and Techniques*, 4th rev. ed. (1982), with extensive bibliography; Hilaire Hiler, *The Painter's Pocket Book of Methods and Materials*, 3rd ed. rev. by Colin Hayes (1970); Kurt Herberts, *The Complete Handbook of Artist's Techniques* (1958; trans. from the German); Maria Bazzi, *The Artist's Methods and Materials* (1960; originally published in Italian, 1956), with a bibliography of important treatises on mediums and techniques; Frederic Taubes, *A Guide to Traditional and Modern Painting Methods* (1963); and Max Doerner, *The Materials of the Artist and Their Use in Painting*, rev. ed. (1949, reprinted 1969; originally published in German, 4th ed., 1933). For discussion of tempera, see the appropriate sections in Daniel V. Thompson, *The Materials of Medieval Painting* (1936; reprinted as *Materials and Techniques of Medieval Painting*, 1956). Watercolour painting is treated in Walter Koschatzky, *Watercolor: History and Technique* (1970; originally published in German, 1969). For treatment of ink painting, see Fei Ch'eng Wu, *Brush Drawing in the Chinese Manner* (1957); and Osvald Síren, *Chinese Painting: Leading Masters and Principles*, 7 vol. (1973). Fred

Gettings, *Polymer Painting Manual* (1971), is a thorough and well-illustrated guide to acrylic painting. Works on other mediums include Jean Guichard-Melli, *Matisse Paper Cutouts* (1984; originally published in French, 1983); and Harriet Janis and Rudi Blesh, *Collage*, rev. ed. (1967).

Forms: William G. Archer, *Indian Miniatures* (1960), and *Indian Paintings from the Punjab Hills: A Survey and History of Pahari Miniature Painting* (1973); Mark Zebrowski, *Deccani Painting* (1983); Janet Woodbury Adams, *Decorative Folding Screens: In the West from 1600 to the Present Day* (U.S. title: *Decorative Folding Screens: 400 Years in the Western World*, 1982); Elise Grilli, *The Art of the Japanese Screen* (1971); Roselee Goldberg, *Performance: From Futurism to the Present*, 3rd ed. (2011); and Adrian Henri, *Environments and Happenings* (U.S. title: *Total Art: Environments, Happenings, and Performance*, 1974).

History and Appreciation: Acton, Mary. *Learning to Look at Paintings,* 2nd ed. (Routledge, 2009). Barker, P.C. *Short Lessons in Art History: Artists and Their Work,* rev. and updated (Walch, 2002). Brommer, G.F. *Discovering Art History,* 4th ed. (Davis, 2007). Chelsea House. *Encyclopedia of Art for Young People* (Chelsea House, 2008). Dickins, Rosie, and Griffith, Mari. *The Usborne Introduction to Art,* new ed. (Usborne, 2009). Janson, H.W., and Janson, A.F. *History of Art for Young People,* 6th ed. (Abrams, 2003). Kleiner, F.S. *Gardner's Art Through the Ages: A Concise Global History,* 2nd ed. (Wadsworth/Cengage, 2009).Sayre, Henry. *Cave*

Paintings to Picasso: The Inside Scoop on 50 Art Masterpieces (Chronicle, 2004).Sturgis, Alexander, ed. *Understanding Paintings: Themes in Art Explored and Explained* (Beazley, 2003).Wilkins, D.G., ed. *The Collins Big Book of Art: From Cave Art to Pop Art* (Collins, 2005).

Imagery: E.H. Gombrich, *Art and Illusion*, 4th ed. (1972); Gyorgy Kepes (ed.), *Sign, Image, Symbol* (1966); Leon M. Zolbrod, *Haiku Painting* (1983); Lucy R. Lippard *et al., Pop Art* (1960, rev. ed. 1970); and J.H. Matthews, *Eight Painters: The Surrealist Context* (1982).

Subject Matter: Howard Daniel, *Encyclopedia of Themes and Subjects in Painting* (1971), a concise survey of Western mythological and religious subjects; David Rosand, *Painting in Cinquecento Venice* (1982); Svetlana Alpers, *The Art of Describing: Dutch Art in the Seventeenth Century* (1983); Norman Bryson, *World and Image: French Painting of the Ancient Régime* (1982); Michael Levey, *The Painter Depicted: Painters as a Subject in Painting* (1982); John Pope-Hennessy, *The Portrait in the Renaissance* (1966, reissued 1979), includes interpretive discussions of the works and extracts from the artists' letters; Kenneth Clark, *Landscape into Art* (1949, reissued 1975); A. Richard Turner, *The Vision of Landscape in Renaissance Italy* (1966, reprinted 1974); Joseph S. Czestochowski, *The American Landscape Tradition* (1982); Roger Boulet, *The Canadian Earth: Landscape Paintings by the Group of Seven* (1982); Michael Jacobs, *Nude Painting* (1979); and Kenneth Clark, *The Nude: A Study of Ideal Art* (1976).

Symbolism: Erwin Panofsky, *Studies in Iconology* (1939, reissued 1972), and *Meaning in the Visual Arts* (1955, reprinted 1982); F.D.K. Bosch, *The Golden Germ* (1960); Carl G. Jung *et al., Man and His Symbols* (posthumous ed. 1964, reprinted 1979), with excellent illustrations; Rudolf Wittkower, *Allegory and the Migration of Symbols* (1977), includes Eastern imagery; Paul Frankl, *The Gothic: Literary Sources and Interpretations Through Eight Centuries* (1960); George Ferguson, *Signs and Symbols in Christian Art* (1954, reprinted 1973); Joan Evans, *Monastic Iconography in France: From the Renaissance to the Revolution* (1970); and Jitendra Nath Banerjea, *The Development of Hindu Iconography*, 2nd rev. ed. (1956, reprinted 1974).

Techniques, Materials, and Methods: G.F. Brommer and N.K. Kinne, *Exploring Painting,* 2nd ed. (2003); Serge Clément and Marina Kamena, *The Joy of Art: A Creative Guide for Beginning Painters* (2000); Diane Edison, *Dynamic Color Painting for the Beginner* (2008); Betty Edwards, *The New Drawing on the Right Side of the Brain,* expanded and updated ed. (2008); Antonella Fuga, *Artists' Techniques and Materials* (2006); Anthony Hodge, *Painting* (2008); Simon Jennings, *The New Artist's Manual: The Complete Guide to Painting and Drawing Materials and Techniques* (2006); and Lucy Watson, and others, *Complete Drawing and Painting Handbook* (2009).

Writings: Irma A. Richter (ed.), *Selections from the Notebooks of Leonardo da Vinci* (1952, reprinted 1977), illustrated; Giorgio Vasari, *Vasari on*

Technique, ed. by G. Baldwin Brown, trans. by Louisa A. Maclehose (1907, reprinted 1961); *The Mustard Seed Garden Manual of Painting, 1679–1701*, included in Mai-mai Sze, *The Tao of Painting*, 2nd ed., 2 vol. (1963); Elizabeth G. Holt (ed.), *A Documentary History of Art*, 2nd ed., 3 vol. (1957–65); John Rewald (ed.), *Cézanne's Letters*, 5th ed. (1982); Vincent Van Gogh, *The Complete Letters of Vincent van Gogh*, 2nd ed., 3 vol. (1978); Fernand Léger, *Functions of Painting*, ed. by Edward F. Fry (1973; originally published in French, 1965); Robert Delaunay and Sonia Delaunay, *The New Art of Color*, ed. by Arthur A. Cohen (1978); Robert Motherwell (ed.), *The Dada Painters and Poets: An Anthology*, 2nd ed. (1981); Marcel Jean (ed.), *The Autobiography of Surrealism* (1980); Wassily Kandinsky, *Kandinsky, Complete Writings on Art*, 2 vol., ed. by Kenneth C. Lindsay and Peter Vergo (1982), with the original illustrations; Paul Klee, *Pedagogical Sketchbook* (1953, reprinted 1977; originally published in German, 1925), *On Modern Art* (1948, reprinted 1966; originally published in German, 1945), *The Thinking Eye*, ed. by Jürg Spiller (1961, reprinted 1969; originally published in German, 1956), and *The Diaries of Paul Klee, 1898–1918*, ed. by Felix Klee (1964, reissued 1968; originally published in German, 1957); Marcel Duchamp, *The Essential Writings of Marcel Duchamp: Salt Seller*, ed. by Michel Sanouillet and Elmer Peterson (1975; originally published in French, 1958), and *Marcel Duchamp, Notes*, ed. by Paul Matisse (1983); Henri Matisse, *Notes of a Painter*, included in Alfred H. Barr, *Matisse: His Art and His Public* (1951, reprinted 1966); Edward

F. Fry, *Cubism* (1966, reprinted 1978; trans. from the French and German); Pierre Daix, *Cubists and Cubism* (1982; originally published in French, 1982); Pablo Picasso, *Picasso on Art: A Selection of Views*, comp. by Dore Ashton (1972); Katharine Kuh, *The Artist's Voice: Talks with Seventeen Artists* (1962); and *The New York School*, foreword by Maurice Tuchman (1970), with an extensive bibliography.

ART CONSERVATION

Valuable general accounts of the field are contained in *Art and Archaeology Technical Abstracts* (semiannual), published by the International Institute for Conservation of Historic and Artistic Work, London. Other general examinations include Andrew Oddy (W.A. Oddy) (ed.), *The Art of the Conservator* (1992); James Beck and Michael Daley, *Art Restoration: The Culture, the Business, and the Scandal* (1993, reprinted 1996); and Nicholas Stanley Price, M. Kirby Talley, Jr., and Alesandra Melucco Vaccaro (eds.), *Historical and Philosophical Issues in the Conservation of Cultural Heritage* (1996). See also John M.A. Thompson et al. (eds.), *The Manual of Curatorship: A Guide to Museum Practice*, 2nd ed. (1992); and Garry Thomson, *The Museum Environment*, 2nd ed. (1986, reprinted 1998). Up-to-the-moment information on specific topics can be found at the Web site for the American Institute for Conservation of Historic and Artistic Works, http://aic.stanford.edu; and the Web site for the International Centre for the Study of the Preservation and Restoration of Cultural Property, http://www.iccrom.org.General studies of issues related to paintings can be found in Helmut Ruhemann, *The Cleaning of Paintings*, with a comprehensive bibliography by Joyce Plesters (1968, reissued 1982); Anthony E. Werner, *The Conservation of Antiquities and Works of Art*, 2nd ed. (1971, reissued 1976); Harold J. Plenderleith, Norman Brommelle, and Perry Smith (eds.), *Conservation and Restoration of Pictorial Art* (1976); David Bomford, *Conservation of Paintings* (1997); Knut Nicolaus, *The Restauration of Paintings* (1999), ed. by Christine Westphal, trans. from German; and Great Britain, National Gallery, *National Gallery Technical Bulletin* (annual). A study of painting on wood is Norman Brommelle, Anne Moncrieff, and Perry Smith (eds.), *Conservation of Wood in Painting and the Decorative Arts* (1978). A study of wall paintings is Paolo Mora, Laura Mora, and Paul Philippot, *Conservation of Wall Paintings* (1984; originally published in French, 1977). Studies of works on paper include Francis W. Dolloff and Roy L. Perkinson, *How to Care for Works of Art on Paper*, 4th ed. (1985); Anne F. Clapp, *Curatorial Care of Works of Art on Paper: Basic Procedures for Paper Preservation*, 3rd rev. ed. (1978, reissued 1987); and Chris Foster, Annette Manick, and Roy L. Perkinson, *Matting and Framing Works of Art on Paper* (1994).

GIACOMO BALLA

S.K. de Rola, *Balla* (1983); Maurizio Fagiolo dell'Arco, *Balla: The Futurist* (1987); Susan Barnes Robinson,

Giacomo Balla: Divisionism and Futurism, 1871–1912 (1981).

COLOUR

Isaac Newton, *Optics; or, A Treatise of the Reflexions, Refractions, Inflexions, and Colours of Light*, 4th ed. (1730, reissued 1979), the beginnings of the scientific study of colour; Johann Wolfgang von Goethe, *Goethe's Theory of Colours* (1840, reissued 1975; originally published in German, 1810), with excellent observations explained by an untenable theory; David L. MacAdam (ed.), *Sources of Color Science* (1970), covering theories developed in all periods but omitting Goethe and including only a little Newton; Ralph Merrill Evans, *An Introduction to Color* (1948, reissued 1965), an authoritative, highly readable introduction, with emphasis on technical applications; and Enid Verity, *Color Observed* (1980), a readable general introduction. A bibliography of colour studies is given in Mary Buckley, *Color Theory: A Guide to Information Sources* (1975). Current research on the subject, together with discussions of applications, is found in the magazines *Color Research and Application* (quarterly), *Inter-Society Color Council News* (bimonthly), and *Journal of the Optical Society of America; Part A, Optics and Image Science* (monthly).

Physics and chemistry of colour: R. Daniel Overheim and David L. Wagner, *Light and Color* (1982), a brief survey; Francis A. Jenkins and Harvey E. White, *Fundamentals of Optics*, 4th ed. (1976); Leslie E.

Orgel, *An Introduction to Transition-Metal Chemistry: Ligand-Field Theory*, 2nd ed. (1966); and Keith McLaren, *The Colour Science of Dyes and Pigments* (1983), authoritative intermediate to advanced texts. Kurt Nassau, *The Physics and Chemistry of Color: The Fifteen Causes of Color* (1983), is a comprehensive up-to-date treatment.

Perception of colour: G. Hugh Begbie, *Seeing and the Eye: An Introduction to Vision* (1969, reprinted 1973), a survey for the general reader; Gerald S. Wasserman, *Color Vision: An Historical Introduction* (1978); and Tom N. Cornsweet, *Visual Perception* (1970), more detailed treatments; Ralph Merrill Evans, *The Perception of Color* (1974); and Robert M. Boynton, *Human Color Vision* (1979), comprehensive advanced texts. Edward C. Carterette and Morton P. Friedman (eds.), *Handbook of Perception*, vol. 5 (1975), contains 12 chapters, written at the advanced level, on all aspects of colour perception.

Colour in art: Samuel J. Williamson and Herman Z. Cummins, *Light and Color in Nature and Art* (1983), a readable, wide-ranging intermediate-level textbook; Johannes Itten, *The Art of Color: The Subjective Experience and Objective Rationale of Color* (1961, reprinted 1973; originally published in German, 1961), an exposition of an influential aesthetic theory; M.E. Chevreul, *The Principles of Harmony and Contrast of Colors and Their Applications to the Arts* (1854, reissued 1981; originally published in French, 1839), with notes by Faber Birren; Faber Birren, *Principles of Color: A Review of Past Traditions and Modern Theories of Color Harmony* (1969), an introduction, and his

History of Color in Painting: With New Principles of Color Expression (1965), an authoritative treatment; and George A. Agoston, *Color Theory and Its Application in Art and Design* (1979), a broad review valuable as a reference work.

ARTHUR DOVE

Barbara Haskell, *Arthur Dove* (1974); Ann Lee Morgan, *Arthur Dove: Life and Work, with a Catalogue Raisonné* (1984); Debra Bricker Balken, William C. Agee, and Elizabeth Hutton Turner, *Arthur Dove: A Retrospective* (1997).

KEITH HARING

Exhibition catalogues include Illinois State University, University Galleries, *Keith Haring: Future Primeval* (1990); Germano Celant (ed.), *Keith Haring* (1992); Elisabeth Sussman, *Keith Haring* (1997); and Götz Adriani (ed.), *Keith Haring: Heaven and Hell* (2001; originally published in German, 2001). John Gruen, *Keith Haring: The Authorized Biography* (1991); and Alexandra Kolossa, *Keith Haring, 1958–1990: A Life for Art* (2004), are among the biographies.

KALI

David Kinsley, *The Sword and the Flute: Kālī and Kṛṣṇa: Dark Visions of the Terrible and the Sublime in Hindu Mythology*, 2nd ed. (2000), and *Hindu*

Goddesses: Visions of the Divine Feminine in the Hindu Religious Tradition (1986, reissued 1997), are good introductions to traditions associated with Kali.

JOHN MARIN

Larry Curry, *John Marin, 1870–1953* (1970); Sheldon Reich, *John Marin: A Stylistic Analysis and Catalogue Raisonné*, 2 vol. (1970); Barbara Rose, *John Marin: The 291 Years* (1998).

REMBRANDT VAN RIJN

Early commentaries on Rembrandt's art can be found in Constantijn Huygens's autobiography of his youth (*c.* 1630), as well as in writings by Joachim von Sandrart (1675), Samuel van Hoogstraten (1678), Andries Pels (1681), Filippo Baldinucci (1686), and Gérard de Lairesse (1707), which are reproduced and discussed in Seymour Slive, *Rembrandt and His Critics, 1630–1730* (1953).

Rembrandt's ideas on art and contemporary reflections on these ideas are examined in J.A. Emmens, *Rembrandt en de regels van de kunst*, vol. 10 in *Orbis artium* (1968), reissued as vol. 2 of *Verzameld werk*, 4 vol. (1979), a work that puts into perspective the image of Rembrandt that was created by the 17th-century Classicistic critics and that continued to influence scholarship well into the 20th century, with a summary in English. Sources that discuss Rembrandt and the earlier tradition include Kenneth Clark, *Rembrandt and the Italian Renaissance* (1966); and B.P.J. Broos, *Index in the Formal Sources of Rembrandt's Art* (1997).

Works and particular subjects are discussed in E. Haverkamp-Begemann, *Rembrandt, the Nightwatch* (1982); Cynthia Schneider, *Rembrandt's Landscapes: Drawings and Prints* (1990); Ann Jensen Adams (ed.), *Rembrandt's Bathsheba Reading King David's Letter* (1998); Christopher White and Quentin Buvelot (eds.), *Rembrandt by Himself*, exhib. cat. (1999); and Julia Lloyd Williams (ed.), *Rembrandt's Women*, exhib. cat. (2001).

Rembrandt's painting technique is the subject of David Bomford, Christopher Brown, and Ashok Roy, *Art in the Making: Rembrandt* (1988); Ernst van de Wetering, *Rembrandt: The Painter at Work* (1997, reissued 2000); and Karin Groen, "An Investigation of the Use of Binding Medium by Rembrandt: Chemical Analyses and Rheology," *Zeitschrift für Kunsttechnologie und Konservierung* 11:207–227 (1997).

GEORGES SEURAT

Cesar de Hauke (comp.), *Seurat et son oeuvre,* 2 vol. (1961), is a basic work that serves as a general catalog to the works of Seurat and complements Henri Dorra and John Rewald, *Seurat* (1959). Lucie Cousturier, *Seurat* (1921; 2nd ed. 1926), gives a lively literary portrait (in French) of the man and the painter. This biographical information was enhanced by Gustave Coquiot, *Seurat* (1924), also in French. Other general studies include Daniel C. Rich, *Seurat and the Evolution of "La Grande Jatte"* (1935, reprinted 1969); Jacques de Laprade, *Georges Seurat* (1945, reissued as *Seurat,* 1951); Meyer Schapiro, "New Light on Seurat," *Art News,* 57:22–24, 44–45, 52 (1958); Anthony Blunt, *Seurat,* with an essay by Roger Fry (1965); John Russell, *Seurat* (1965); and Pierre Courthion, *Georges Seurat* (1968). On Seurat's technique and aesthetic theories, Jules Christophe, "Georges Seurat," in *Les Hommes d'aujourd'hui,* vol. 8 (1890), is basic.

JOHANNES VERMEER

Important to any understanding of modern assessments of Vermeer are the groundbreaking writings on the artist by W. Bürger (pseudonym of Théophile Thoré): especially "Van der Meer de Delft," *Gazette des Beaux-Arts,* vol. 21 (1866). More-recent studies of Vermeer's life and work, with catalogs of his paintings, include P.T.A. Swillens, *Johannes Vermeer: Painter of Delft, 1632–1675* (1950); Albert Blankert, *Vermeer of Delft: Complete Edition of the Paintings* (1978); Lawrence Gowing, *Vermeer,* 3rd ed. (1997); and Arthur K. Wheelock, Jr., *Jan Vermeer,* new ed. (1970), and *Vermeer: The Complete Works* (1997). Arthur K. Wheelock, Jr. (ed.), *Johannes Vermeer* (1995), the catalog accompanying the 1995–96 exhibition held at the National Gallery of Art in Washington, D.C., and at the Mauritshuis, The Hague, includes much new information about the artist's life and work, including contemporary assessments of his paintings and the methods he used for creating perspective. A well-written historical narrative of Vermeer's life is Anthony Bailey, *Vermeer: A View of Delft* (2001).

Specialized studies: A variety of approaches to studying the artist and his oeuvre are contained in Ivan Gaskell and Michiel Jonker (eds.), *Vermeer Studies* (1998); and Wayne E. Franits (ed.), *The Cambridge Companion to Vermeer* (2001). Daniel Arasse, *Vermeer: Faith in Painting* (1994); and Ivan Gaskell, *Vermeer's Wager: Speculations on Art History, Theory, and Art Museums* (2000), are both ostensibly focused around particular paintings, but they actually encompass broader themes related to Vermeer.

Extensive studies of 17th-century Delft, specifically in relationship to Vermeer, include John Michael Montias, *Artists and Artisans in Delft: A Socio-Economic Study of the Seventeenth Century* (1982), and *Vermeer and His Milieu* (1989). Also noteworthy are Walter Liedtke, *A View of Delft: Vermeer and His Contemporaries* (2000); and Walter Liedtke (ed.), *Vermeer and the Delft School* (2001), a catalog accompanying an exhibit at the Metropolitan Museum of Art in New York City and at the National Gallery in London.

Vermeer's painting techniques are discussed in Maryan W. Ainsworth et al., *Art and Autoradiography: Insights into the Genesis of Paintings by Rembrandt, Van Dyck, and Vermeer* (1982); and Arthur K. Wheelock, Jr., *Perspective, Optics, and Delft Artists Around*

1650 (1977), and *Vermeer and the Art of Painting* (1995); and Philip Steadman, *Vermeer's Camera: Uncovering the Truth Behind the Masterpieces* (2001). A video that focuses on Vermeer's techniques, including his use of the camera obscura, is the National Gallery of Art, Washington, D.C., *Vermeer: Master of Light* (2001), narrated by Meryl Streep.